Family Business and Responsible Wealth Ownership

Preparing the Next Generation

Editor
Iraj Ispahani

Managing director
Sian O'Neill

Family Business and Responsible Wealth Ownership: Preparing the Next Generation
is published by

Globe Law and Business Ltd
3 Mylor Close
Horsell
Woking
Surrey GU21 4DD
United Kingdom
Tel: +44 20 3745 4770
www.globelawandbusiness.com

Printed and bound in Great Britain by Ashford Colour Press Ltd

Family Business and Responsible Wealth Ownership: Preparing the Next Generation

ISBN 9781787425026
EPUB ISBN 9781787425033
Adobe PDF ISBN 9781787425040

Table of contents

Preface

Iraj Ispahani
Ispahani Advisory

When I was invited to become contributing editor of this Special Report, I thought that it presented a few worthwhile challenges which, if addressed, could result in the creation of a holistic and timely repository for the rising next generation in this pandemic-stricken era. Over the past year, all generations have experienced increased anxiety and become more aware of their mortality. The ensuing conversations within families about their health and wealth have become more explicit. How can the rising next generation make sense of a world facing upheaval on a scale not seen since World War II? What do they really need to know? *Family Business and Responsible Wealth Ownership: Preparing the Next Generation* aims to develop a shared mindset and a better understanding between generations, focusing in particular on matters from the perspective of the next generation to enable them to help themselves lead meaningful lives.

Family businesses and wealth owners must contend with manifold challenges today, including increased government interventionism, business disruption, technology-driven change, international conflicts and the climate crisis. The pandemic has also underscored the need for all businesses to apply more sustainable business practices and a few forward-looking family businesses are embracing circularity. Circularity means avoiding waste – not just of natural resources, but also of the human resources within families, including family members who are not directly involved in the family business, but who have a stake in the future and who need to support those in more active roles. In addition, the move in recent years to the greater transparency of mid-shore and onshore jurisdictions and the disclosure enabled by the Common Reporting Standard have increased the scrutiny of wealth owners by governments, tax authorities, regulators and the media. All of these changes further complicate the processes of creating, retaining and transitioning wealth. They also underline the increasing need for dialogue between wealth and business owners, who are so important to economies, and governments and other stakeholders.

Wealth and business-owning families are aware of an increased focus in society on responsible capitalism and throughout the pandemic the private sector has played its part – often below the radar – in supporting local communities and beyond. But there is much more to be done. Today there remains the very real risk of increased inequalities caused by the pandemic, both within the same country, between 'knowledge workers' and manual and frontline workers, and between countries – those that have the COVID-19 vaccine and those that don't; those with governments that can hand out money and those without.

Families must in parallel address internal issues which can become greater derailers than the challenges of the external environment. Families must ensure that they themselves are sustainable. Family continuity can be undermined without adequate preparation for succession. In thinking about the content of this book, I focused on aspects of this preparation that the next generation particularly needs. First, I wanted to include a range of themes, including finding one's purpose; developing resilience; the benefits of mentoring; preparing women for wealth; social media use and reputation management; understanding asset protection structures; encouraging entrepreneurship and understanding the purpose of capital. They are all, in my experience, relevant to the rising next generation in their formative years and indeed later. Families need advisers, but it is the families themselves that need to understand their own structures and the checks and balances required.

Second, I thought the tone was important too: not prescriptive or hierarchical, but open and supportive. The rising next generation are too often told what to do, which can be off-putting. My intention with this Special Report is to take a practical approach that encourages the rising next generation to listen, learn and act as needed. To make the choices that are right for them. To take responsibility for their futures by engaging with their families' expectations. The rising next generation are the future of those families and should be better understood and supported so that family human capital is not taken for granted, wasted or overlooked. This, in my experience, happens rather too often and is best avoided. It is also important to develop clear roles for 'family elders' whose experience can help in mentoring the younger generations.

Third, I wanted to bring together leading experts from around the world with decades of practical experience working across cultures with wealth-owning families on an intergenerational basis, together with the perspectives of the lived experience of business-owning families.

I would like to take this opportunity to thank all of my distinguished fellow contributors for their thoughtful and insightful chapters: Jed Emerson and Paul Hokemeyer in the United States; Charlie Bain, Ed Lee, Jessica McGawley and Caroline Underwood in the United Kingdom; Stefan Liniger in Switzerland; and Philip Marcovici in Hong Kong. Our thanks to Nicolette Fourie for driving the overall process with infectious enthusiasm, and to Sian O'Neill at Globe Law and Business, for her sagacity and encouragement. I am indebted to my wife Eva for encouraging me greatly throughout the realisation of this project and for her considerable wisdom and perspective on the issues covered in this Special Report.

London, June 2021

I. Managing your context today and finding and deploying purpose

Iraj Ispahani
Ispahani Advisory

1. Purpose and the post-pandemic world

The COVID-19 pandemic has encouraged many of us to think about our role in life and our sense of purpose. The pandemic has signalled a time to reflect and rethink who we are and what we stand for. Never before have we been on such a steep learning curve, and so keenly reminded of our mortality and the importance of assessing, managing and mitigating those risks that we are aware of. The pandemic has challenged *modi operandi* around the world, including the ways that nations function; the relationships between business, government and civil society; and our attitudes about what we value in society. Some people will continue much as before; but many, particularly in the rising next generation[1] of business and wealth-owning families – women and men in their 20s, 30s and 40s – will be determined to be heard more clearly and feel a greater sense of urgency to contribute more to society. These individuals are, of course, just a small subset of a much wider rising next generation global cohort; but they represent an influential privileged subset with access to the levers to drive and deliver change for the wider benefit and inclusion of the many. This subset of the rising next generation is asking, "Why am I here? Who am I? What are my goals and aspirations? Am I deserving? How can I contribute?" Some already have a well-defined sense of direction; while others may well find it on a more iterative basis by trying out different approaches. As we think about the need to adapt our society via a new social contract, this is an opportunity to shape the future. Awareness of societal disparities drove my commitment to purpose in the past, encapsulated in my work with Seeing is Believing (SiB) and Shakespeare's Globe, described later in this chapter. I have also been reflecting on the way ahead.

Before the pandemic, income and wealth inequality was already driving change on the global political and tax landscape. Brexit uncertainty in Europe, Hong Kong protests and political divisions in the United States were worrying those families that think in generations rather than in years or decades. The Industrial Revolution (which heralded the advent of fossil fuel burning) provided the foundation for how the pre-pandemic economy operated. We must now use our knowledge and tools to build a more circular economy that is fit for the post-pandemic 21st century, and our thinking and behaviours must adapt to this new operating environment. The diluted linkage between business and society must be reinvigorated. Profit maximisation must be balanced with a corporate purpose, with businesses proactively considering the needs of their wider stakeholder group and not just their shareholders. B corporations are a good example of companies that are already trying to address this. With significant business ownership of listed entities now held through funds and passive

"We must now use our knowledge and tools to build a more circular economy that is fit for the post-pandemic 21st century, and our thinking and behaviours must adapt to this new operating environment."

vehicles, the ability of these shareholders to make their votes count and encourage corporates to reprioritise will be an important feature of this changing landscape.

It is tempting to talk about getting 'back to normal', but we are most unlikely to go back to the way things were. In fact, going 'back to normal' is also not what many millions of people aspire to or deserve, as Dame Polly Courtice, founder director of the Cambridge Institute of Sustainability Leadership, has wisely observed: "For many, the current system has failed to deliver health, wellbeing, and prosperity. Now that the lack of resilience in the 'old' system has been revealed, alongside our ability to mobilise vast sums of money and resources for vaccines when the economy is at risk, expectations will have been raised about what else is now possible in the face of other crises."[2]

During lockdowns around the world, families across generations have reflected on their wider purpose. What more can they do in the face of the stark inequalities which the pandemic highlighted in their particular communities, countries or regions? Sustainable practices and addressing climate change have understandably risen on the personal and corporate agenda. So what can the rising next generation learn from history as they look ahead and try to harness their purpose? History reminds us of the disruption that occurs when revolutions happen, borders are redrawn and wars develop. Notable examples of geopolitical disruption include the general expropriations which occurred following the Mexican Revolution, the Bolshevik Revolution, the Nazi German invasion of Europe and the Cuban Revolution. In every instance, assets – including key industrial and commercial assets and land – were seized from private citizens by governments, in some cases by being declared abandoned property. History tells us that things can change fast and nothing should be taken for granted.

At a global level, what about war and conflict today? It's a disturbing picture. According to the International Committee of the Red Cross[3] (ICRC), there are more conflict zones globally today than ever before. These 35 conflict zones are all located in emerging and frontier markets, in both rural and urban settings, resulting in a huge number of displaced people both within and across borders. Migrants and refugees are among the groups worst impacted by the pandemic. The ICRC has highlighted the millions of people living in conflict zones around the world, with COVID-19 an additional threat to them. In many of these countries, health systems and other vital infrastructure have been destroyed by war. One of the lessons that the ICRC has learned from the outbreak of Ebola in Liberia is that when all attention, finances and resources are focused on one viral disease, you risk ignoring other areas, such as malaria treatment or primary healthcare. So while the world's focus has been on the current pandemic because it is a shared, borderless experience – a common enemy that we all face – there are many ongoing conflicts that are having devastating effects on individual countries and regions, which should not be forgotten.

2. Climate, conflict, community

The linkage of climate, conflict and communities is not widely understood, but is significant and worth reflecting on – particularly in the run-up to the 26th UN Climate Change Conference of the Parties (COP 26), which the United Kingdom will host in Glasgow from 1–12 November 2021. The summit will bring parties together to accelerate action towards the goals of the Paris Agreement and the UN Framework Convention on Climate Change. This decade we are now in was initially earmarked for getting our climate on track for net zero by 2050 and making progress on the UN Sustainable Development Goals (SDGs), but will now play out in a new, as yet undefined, framework. Mark Carney, former governor of the Bank of England, hopes that the COP 26 conference "can be the watershed in a new, more inclusive and sustainable global economic system".[4]

Over the years, the ICRC has witnessed how the daily lives of people enduring situations of armed conflict are made difficult not only by the violence they experience, but also by climate risks and environmental degradation. According to Robert Mardini,[5] director general of the ICRC, the conflict, droughts and floods experienced for decades in countries such as Somalia and Afghanistan have repeatedly threatened people's food security and forced many to relocate. In many cases, conflict also directly harms the very ecosystems on which people rely for their survival. People are being affected by armed conflict and climate change, says Mardini. Sixty per cent of the 20 countries considered to be most vulnerable to climate change by the ND-Gain Index[6] are also sites of armed conflict. This is partly because of their geographical location; but mostly because conflicts increase the fragility of institutions, essential services, infrastructure and governance which are fundamental to people's resilience to a changing climate and environment.

Looking beyond COVID-19, one of our great challenges in the developing world is the pace of urbanisation and preparing children today for their part in the workforce of the future – in Bangladesh alone, 11 million people move annually to the cities. Asia-Pacific has 60% of the world's young people and 10.5% of those are unemployed, so education and employment are critical and inextricably linked. In sub-Saharan Africa, the projected 40% decline in agricultural jobs is also fuelling a move to the cities. This is something which UNICEF, where I serve as a UK adviser, is addressing through its Generation Unlimited programme for young people.[7] The needs and expectations of the rising next generation should be uppermost in all our minds as

"One of our great challenges in the developing world is the pace of urbanisation and preparing children today for their part in the workforce of the future."

we think through our purpose and what matters today. Why are we doing something? Who are we doing it for? What is the investment required and time horizon to effect change? How will we measure the difference we hope to make?

3. The path to finding my own purpose

I have painted a picture of a challenged, fractured world and highlighted some of the issues which I am personally concerned about. Inevitably, there is much to be done and many ways in which to contribute. The pandemic has made us focus on what we value as we look ahead. It is with this context and thinking about the rising next generation who are considering these issues that I turn to some reflections on my own journey in life and the events which shaped my perspective, sense of self and purpose.

My initial motivations stem from the charitable endeavours to which I was exposed during my childhood. These instilled in me a personal commitment and enthusiasm to play my part as best I could for the benefit of others. This was not selfless by any means, since most people who volunteer will recognise that volunteering is itself a privilege. For me, the 'Why'[8] was embedded in my formative years; but to find the 'How', I had to chart my own course. Doing nothing was never an option. I think that taking a community-first charitable approach played its part; as did adopting a values-based framework, which my family provided. These informal guidelines provided me with a social compass as I grew up. As a young adult, I started to realise the challenges around creating lasting societal impact, which meant adopting an open learning mindset, being curious and tenacious. I started to learn more about how this could be done in health and education, which I had a particular interest in. As a child, I was made aware of the responsibility that comes with a positive start in life and I have tried to make a difference wherever I have lived. In my case, there was no 'eureka' moment; rather a series of connected influences and experiences from my formative years into early adulthood and beyond – and some serendipity! As we reflect in this Special Report on the world today and how to navigate it from the perspective of the rising next generation, I thought it would be helpful to share my experiences and some of the lessons I learned.

The duties and obligations of responsible business and wealth ownership are at the core of my thinking. For me, the definition of family wealth encompasses human, social, intellectual and financial capital. The linkages between business and society were clear to me from my childhood, and I have tried to develop these linkages over the years by creating wider awareness of issues and building bridges with communities. You may well have the disposition and interest in discovering your purpose; but how can you, as a member of the rising next generation, find and define your own path – something that works for you personally? I will share how I found mine.

The theme of partnering – developing the right ways to encourage much-needed societal change, particularly in emerging markets – is one that I increasingly focused on. Starting from a point of asking, "What can I do to help others?", I asked myself what more I could do to accelerate change and deliver impact to some of the critical issues that the world was facing. I knew that as an individual, I could only play a small part as a supporter, a fundraiser, a mentor and a communicator; but as I lived and learned, I saw how this could best be realised. I was purposeful. I wanted to move beyond personal charity. I wanted to develop my voice for some of the causes which had resonance with me. As Jed Emerson[9] writes so eloquently in Chapter VIII: "When we think about impact, most likely we think about it as something that happens to the other; something that we do to other people or communities ... But impact is about more than what we might do to others ... In our efforts to make a positive contribution through the deployment of our capital, in our focus on generating positive blended value, we open up the opportunity for us to connect, to reflect, to engage; and in that process, to be transformed ourselves." This for me encapsulates the journey towards delivering meaningful change which I embarked on.

I took some personal risk when I co-founded an online communications business in London during the technology bubble of the early 2000s and through this experience developed respect for entrepreneurs as they try to manage risk/reward trade-offs. James Chen of the Chen Yat Sen Family Foundation, and a highly respected campaigner for eye health, is concerned[10] that philanthropy – particularly institutional philanthropy – is averse to risk. He suggests that if you are an agent of capital rather than an owner, you start to suffer the institutional paralysis that often afflicts governments. This is the wrong approach, he says: impact is proportional to risk, so if you want to have impact, you have to take risks. The implication for the rising next generation is that while they may be less constrained than institutional-led philanthropy, they should still do their due diligence homework thoroughly on established organisations or impact ventures. A sobering statistic is that fewer than half of all impact enterprises last more than a year.

The organisations that I became involved with decades ago are today an enriching part of my life. SiB is now part of a global movement; and at Shakespeare's Globe, where I served as a board trustee for a dozen years, we are all part of a big international family. At the outset, I tried to avoid taking a compartmentalised view based on the singular objectives, however laudable, of individual charities and non-governmental organisations (NGOs) – that is just a starting point. What becomes both more challenging and more interesting is to stand back and think holistically about the issues themselves and how more transformative change can be achieved together. I recall the words of the great Indian independence leader, Mahatma Gandhi,[11] who observed: "Be the change that you wish to see in the world." Sometimes, in my experience, this change is best achieved by encouraging more organisations to work together and not compete unnecessarily. Fragmentation of effort leads to wasted resources. Encouraging more public sector and private sector cooperation remains vital. The rapid pace of COVID-19 vaccine development, production and distribution has exemplified this recently. The speed with which governments, scientists, the health service, corporations, regulators and international NGOs (eg, the World Health Organization and UNICEF on the Covax Fund) combined forces highlights that when there is a sufficiently urgent issue to be tackled, different stakeholders can and do rise to the occasion.

Private sector/INGO partnership

A successful partnership that I witnessed, in my role as an independent trustee of the Standard Chartered Foundation, was the agile collaboration between UNICEF and Standard Chartered Bank, which exemplifies the multiplier effect you need during a major crisis. Standard Chartered made a $5 million donation to UNICEF at the outset of the COVID-19 pandemic for the immediate educational support of vulnerable children across 12 countries in Africa and South Asia. Funding was to focus on the provision of remote education via TV, radio, online and mobile platforms and child protection measures, including alternative care arrangements and family tracing services for children separated from their families due to the pandemic, training for social workers to conduct home visits to vulnerable children for mental health support, and alternative care and protection services for children and parents or caregivers affected by COVID-19.

71.7 million beneficiaries reached... of whom Standard Chartered's donations was enough to support 22 million

Bangladesh	17,466,646	Nepal	21,066
Cameroon	189,293	Myanmar	0*
Côte d'Ivoire	103,215	Pakistan	36,019,973
Ghana	9,177,934	Tanzania	2,500,000
Kenya	34,227	Uganda	2,592,739
Laos	3,599,781	Zambia	62,000

Source: UNICEF/Standard Chartered Progress Report, November 2020.
** Developing remote education resources and securing permissions from education stakeholders in the country has been difficult given the climate; schools in the country have also remained closed.*

Overview of Standard Chartered's impact
Standard Chartered's donation enabled UNICEF to respond to the emerging education and protection needs of children in 12 key countries across Africa and Asia, as highlighted on the map. UNICEF's child protection and education response across the 12 countries could reach 79.4 million children and has already reached 71.7 million beneficiaries. Of these, support from Standard Chartered was enough to reach 31% of the beneficiaries – that's over 22 million people.

UNICEF's scale and reach meant it was able to flex its response to meet humanitarian needs of children as they emerged. In some countries, approvals for remote learning took a long time to secure. In others, UNICEF was able to mobilise almost immediately. In certain countries, UNICEF was able to reach a huge population via television and radio; while in others, the priority turned out to be reaching the most vulnerable communities who could not use or access such technologies, such as the disabled and those in remote regions.

During my childhood, I became aware of two themes which my family had long supported: primary and secondary education for girls and boys, and eye health. My choice in the first instance was to build on the charitable themes that my family had pursued. I had great respect for what they had contributed. My late grandmother, to whom I was close, was a great source of inspiration: a humanitarian and dedicated social worker focusing on baby and child welfare, and a strong advocate for girls' education. It is through her work – including with the International Red Cross in Geneva, for which I remember filling care parcels as a young boy for victims of flood relief – that I started to understand the extent of societal need and disparities, and began to think about ways in which I could also play my part. In 1960, the year of my birth, my great-uncle founded a free eye care dispensary in Dhaka as a small local philanthropy initiative. He could see that societal needs across the country were huge and resolutely backed his idea and scaled it thoughtfully, energetically and generously. This grew into the regionally renowned Ispahani Islamia Eye Hospital and Institute. In 2003, this hospital in Bangladesh became a catalyst for a global programme to address reversible blindness. In some senses it was the pilot light which, once lit, enabled significant impact to be achieved globally in overcoming reversible blindness.

Over the years, I learned the importance of witnessing the work that an organisation does before becoming involved. This demonstrates your genuine interest in what it does and how it delivers. With UNICEF, for instance, I made several trips over a couple of years to Bangladesh from the United Kingdom and visited a range of its projects, from primary and secondary schools in inner city slums to water sanitation and hygiene projects, street children shelters and mother and baby maternity clinics. I became much better informed about the issues in each project, and the funding and governance requirements. When you appreciate the sheer scale of needs in densely populated countries, you also realise how difficult it can be to prioritise and allocate resources in emerging markets. When you visit a project and the people involved, both as project leaders and as local community beneficiaries, you see and hear so much more than a report will ever tell you. Reading a report becomes more meaningful when you understand what is being delivered on the ground. You develop working relationships with local colleagues and witness their commitment. You begin to feel more informed and involved. You learn to ask the right questions when you are sitting around a board or committee table. You learn to trust, but also to probe, challenge and verify.

4. The 'I' and the 'We'

Over the years, I have reflected on the 'I' and the 'We' to see whether they were aligned. In my case, the sectors that I became closely involved in – eye health and education – were consistent with areas that my family had traditionally supported. For me, therefore, this tension between a personal agenda and a family agenda did not represent a challenge; but it can be a significant issue for rising next generation members who wish to pursue causes or hold beliefs that are not consistent with those of their families or family foundations, which often provide the funding. In my view, there has to be accommodation of the 'I' and the 'We' if families are to co-exist happily and flourish. Why should individuals in a family simply subscribe to collective responsibility because it's expected? As Jessica McGawley[12] underlines in her chapter of this Special Report, individuation is to be expected and respected as a source of identity. As Jay Hughes observes: "The whole family's intention being to enhance that individual's process of individuation of happiness – toward the whole family flourishing."[13] This definition of the common interest is vital and it being embedded during one's childhood, adolescence and early adulthood is fundamental. What the common interest is will vary from family to family; but each family must manage its own context by asking two simple questions: "Where did we come from?" and "Where do we want to go?" As Alex Haley,[14] the author of *Roots*, said: "In every conceivable manner, the family is link to our past, bridge to our future."

At what point does the insistence on individualism threaten family unity? For example, if there is a family business, to achieve cohesion, everyone involved needs an understanding of the values that underpin the family business. Sometimes these values have to be updated and redefined so that successive generations feel their relevance, or are at

"Each family must manage its own context by asking two simple questions: 'Where did we come from?' and 'Where do we want to go?'"

least reminded of them. You can base your strategic decisions on these values and use them to encourage the right behaviours. The grandparents' and parents' generations and their advisers must try to ensure that everyone is singing from the same hymn sheet. Values may evolve and change: not so long ago, the world was very patriarchal and hierarchical; but today we have a flatter, more democratic structure which allows and encourages more questioning. This, of course, is more the case in some cultures than in others. The younger generations are not as easily accepting of the approach of previous generations and must buy into any planned transitions within a family enterprise. Families that are clearer on their values, and whose governance frameworks embed and endorse these values, will be more successful in holding their family and business together. Disruption is likely to increase – geopolitically, as already noted; and also driven by technological advances in areas including artificial intelligence. Positive reputations for families and their businesses in this fast-evolving environment will likely be more difficult to maintain, but a shared sense of purpose can add much-needed cohesion and glue.

I will now share my experience of working on a voluntary basis with SiB and Shakespeare's Globe.

Case study: Seeing is Believing – a reversible blindness initiative

In 2006, I met the then group CEO of Standard Chartered Bank, Mervyn Davies, at the Royal Academy in London, who suggested that I become more involved with SiB, the bank's joint initiative with the International Agency for the Prevention of Blindness (IAPB). Mervyn was known for being very persuasive! SiB had begun in 2003, when the bank committed to raise enough money for 28,000 sight-restoring surgeries – one for every member of staff at the time – to celebrate its 150th anniversary. In 2003, Mervyn witnessed a mother have her cataracts removed in Dhaka at the Ispahani Islamia Eye Hospital and Institute and see her children for the first time. He was moved deeply and inspired to do much more for reversible blindness. I was glad to be asked to become more involved, but I wasn't clear how I could contribute, given that I didn't have an ophthalmic or medical background and didn't work at Standard Chartered, whose staff did most of the fundraising. However, eye health was an issue which I had become familiar with as a boy and the SiB mission had great resonance with me. It can be easy to rule oneself out from an opportunity because others appear to be better equipped to contribute; but if you have a passion to do something and are willing to learn, it's surprising how quickly things can fall into place! Sometimes you just have to jump in and learn to swim.

"It can be easy to rule oneself out from an opportunity because others appear to be better equipped to contribute; but if you have a passion to do something and are willing to learn, it's surprising how quickly things can fall into place!"

What struck me in particular was the ambition for scale across emerging markets through leveraging eye health expert NGO partnerships and technology. I knew that more than 75% of all visual impairment could be prevented or cured and 80% of visual impairment was across emerging markets, which the bank also knew and understood particularly well; so the addressable market was huge. I had also heard that for each unsighted child, it takes two or perhaps three sighted adults to help them through life; so there is a clear socio-economic cost. Avoidable blindness and visual impairment are key health issues in emerging markets, impacting access to education and employment opportunities with long-term implications for livelihoods and economic growth. Here are some statistics on the scale of the issue. An estimated 1.35 billion people globally have significant levels of vision loss: 36 million are blind; 217 million have very serious problems seeing distance objects; and 1.1 billion have problems seeing near objects.[15] Some 89% of those affected live in low and middle-income countries. Good vision is pivotal to educational attainment and facilitates participation in the workforce, contributing to economic benefits and a sense of identity. Some estimates state that every $1 invested in eliminating avoidable blindness generates on average $4 of economic gain in emerging economies.[16]

I joined the Advisory Board of SiB as an external member in 2007 and over 14 years, until the end of 2020, contributed to developing a robust governance framework and criteria that facilitated project selection and monitoring, encouraged innovation and supported fundraising. Measuring the impact of individual projects was an objective that initially was challenging to implement, but had to be done and was achieved. At the outset, some projects seeking funding did not understand what key performance indicators were or what we meant by projects being developed with a view to having a sustainable future once bank funding ceased. If they didn't understand this clearly, it would have been difficult to create the requisite accountability. So working with the recipients of funding to help them manage their projects was often a process of patient education and collaboration, done very much in the spirit of partnership. They had often not been through the reporting requirements which were now to be expected. Throughout this period, we had to ensure that all projects were properly supported, which the bank's dedicated staff of volunteers and fundraisers did very helpfully. Providing computers and local training on using software was just one example of how this was delivered on the ground. To support our monitoring function, the IAPB provided an excellent risk register which enabled us to track how funds were being deployed, and any issues arising were generally flagged early by the vigilant and extremely well-informed Sally Crook of the IAPB.

Regular visits to these projects from country CEOs and board members, and advisory board members, were another way to show support and conduct informal due diligence.

Between 2003 and 2020, SiB-funded projects were implemented by international eye health organisations to provide access to affordable and quality eye health services to people in low and middle-income countries. SiB evolved from supporting cataract surgeries at the outset, as mentioned, into a global multi-stakeholder partnership that supports comprehensive eye care, strengthening eye health systems and fostering the development of new technologies across Asia, Africa, the Middle East and South America.

In 2014, SiB invested in nine innovation fund projects to promote innovative solutions towards eye health, including using technology as an accelerator. Peek Vision was one of these projects.

Peek Vision – technology as an accelerator
Andrew Bastawrous, an ophthalmologist, is the founder and CEO of Peek Vision. Peek Vision develops smartphone technology and public health tools to help eye health organisations in delivering more efficient, more effective and more equitable programmes by working with health providers, NGOs and governments.

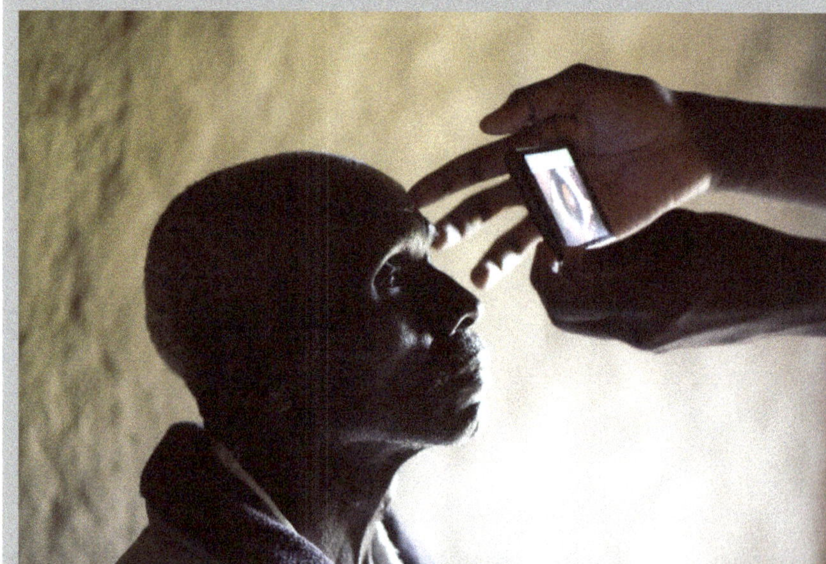

Photo credit: Rolex/Joan Bardeletti

Peek's tools incorporate the clinically validated Peek Acuity smartphone visual acuity test as part of a powerful system for capturing and analysing data from school and community eye health programmes and large-scale surveys.

With Peek, eye health providers can use real-time data to identify gaps and inequalities in their services. People who are hard to reach or who would have been invisible to health workers are made visible, so that nobody is left behind.

Photo credit: Rolex/Joan Bardeletti

Thanks to support from SiB, Peek is being scaled around the globe (seven countries currently), including a nationwide school eye health programme in Botswana, in which every schoolchild in the country is being screened and treated; and programmes in Asia that treat over 1,000 people per day.

In 2018, Standard Chartered celebrated 15 years of SiB at the British Museum and announced that with bank matching, the $100 million fundraising target had been reached two years ahead of schedule. This was a great reflection on the successful fundraising by bank staff around the world, and also underlined what can be achieved through an organisation embracing a cause and supporting it consistently and wholeheartedly over a meaningful period of time. SiB reached 250 million people through 237 projects across 38 low-and middle-income countries. This includes 44 innovation fund projects, such as Peek, to develop pioneering ideas with the potential to transform how eye care is delivered in low-and middle-income countries. During this period, SiB supported 5.1 million sight-restoring surgeries and 7.4 million people were treated for other eye conditions, including glaucoma, diabetic retinopathy and retinopathy of prematurity. SiB dispensed 1.78 million pairs of spectacles and low-vision devices. In addition, 37,000 people were screened for visual impairment. What had started in 2003 with a local cataract-focused initiative with Ispahani Islamia Eye Hospital and Institute in Dhaka had been nurtured, carefully managed and grown well beyond our expectations. SiB is now recognised as a strong model for corporates and NGOs to deliver the SDGs.[17]

For me, the opportunity to be part of an international team delivering this significant global initiative with a great track record has been hugely gratifying. Most importantly, I have become an advocate for eye health. As ever, there remains much to be done in the battle to eradicate reversible blindness around the world and I hope to continue to put my voice to good use.

SHAKESPEARE'S GLOBE

Case study: Shakespeare's Globe – an educational charity

I would also like to share my perspective on realising Sam Wanamaker's vision and the rebuilding of the Globe on London's Bankside. In true Shakespearean fashion, this is the story of one towering hero and a supporting cast of thousands!

I am often asked how I became so deeply involved with the Globe over almost 30 years. My involvement has been purely voluntary and yet the Globe has been integral to my adult life. It's a story that I am delighted to share with you. As a child in Dhaka, I read Shakespeare. When I came to school in England, that early interest in the written word and performance continued to grow. My view was and remains that Shakespeare was a global citizen and not just the quintessential Englishman – a view I shared with Sam.

The Globe was established as an educational charity and its initial focus was very much on the schoolchildren of Southwark, where the Globe is based. In 1997, when the scaffolding in the theatre was removed, the newly painted 'heavens' were revealed. These heavens – the canopy over the stage, in the blues and golds of astrological signs – were paid for by £100,000 raised by schoolchildren. Some 350 schools from 27 countries buried time capsules at the centre of the Globe site through the Globelinks programme. Each school paid £100 to bury a capsule holding mementoes of 20th century school days in the foundations – an indication of the extent to which education is integral to our whole enterprise. We will find out in 2047 what each capsule contains – so patience will be required! As you can see, the Globe from its earliest days 'belonged' to British schoolchildren, especially those from Southwark, where we have our roots. The Globe has a commitment to exploring Elizabethan and Jacobean theatre in the playing conditions under which Shakespeare and his contemporaries originally worked. This principle underlies all its work with schools and universities.

I thought it worth sharing a few pre-pandemic data points on the reach and impact of the Globe. As I write, the current picture for the creative arts is sobering and our collective future depends on the speed with which we can reopen for business and continuing government support through the UK government's Culture Recovery Fund, for which we at the Globe are most grateful.

- With over one million annual visitors, the Globe is recognised as one of the United Kingdom's major cultural and heritage assets.
- The Globe attracts 10% of London's play-going audience, with an annual income of around £25 million.
- More people engage with Shakespeare through the Globe than anywhere else in the world. Every year, over 600,000 people see a production at the Globe or on tour.
- Globe Education works with over 140,000 students each year. It has resident academics leading original research and working with international scholars. It offers a joint MA with King's College London in Shakespeare and English. It still maintains 42% of its tickets for 700 groundlings at £5 and offers 20,000 free tickets to schoolchildren from London and Birmingham.

While I may appear to have become involved in the early stages of the Globe, I was in some senses late to the party when I met Sam in 1991. At the time, all the project had to show for itself was a hole in the ground and considerable bank debts. Sam had been waxing lyrical for almost 25 years about his dream. My friend, the late Dr Diana Devlin, was with Sam from this first phase and she told me about what they faced together, remarking that there were more downs than ups! By the time Diana met him, Sam was already in collaboration with Theo Crosby, the architect who could translate scholars' conjectures into a design for a real building.

Sam Wanamaker Playhouse. Courtesy of Shakespeare's Globe
Photographer: Pete Le May

For much of the journey, the sheer size of Sam's vision was a burden to him. He liked to tilt at windmills! Even in its scaled-down version, he was pursuing the art of the possible instead of the ideal:

Sam began to raise interest in his project by mounting a summer season of plays in a magnificent tent on borrowed land by the river a few hundred yards from the original Globe. It was far more than a theatre season – there was a 6-week summer school, a children's painting competition, a film festival, a concert in Southwark Cathedral and medieval plays in its precincts. The following year – disaster – the tent blew down in a heavy rainstorm, and there was no money to continue. But the project lived on. Sam found an old building nearby which had once been a Bear Garden in Shakespeare's time. He opened a tiny theatre museum there, and that was the flagship of the project for many years, soon becoming an education centre as well because education was always at the heart of Sam's vision. The Museum had a small replica 17th century theatre in it, so much of the work was practical and formed the basis of the extensive education programme we have today.[18]

In 1991, when I was a banker at JP Morgan in London, I was invited to a reception at St James's Palace. My office was in Pall Mall, a mere five minutes' walk away, so I had no excuse for being late or getting stuck in traffic. During the course of the evening, I had the opportunity to meet Sam Wanamaker for the first time. He was charismatic, engaging and easy to bond with. We spoke, we got on and I was, as we say at the Globe, "touched by Sam" – as many others have been over the years. Sharing this conversation was a magnificent older lady with a big grey bun – the redoubtable Anne Ward, former Labour councillor of Southwark and firm friend of the Globe. I was back at my desk at the office next morning when the phone rang at 8:30 am; it was the very same Anne Ward calling to follow up. My lasting impression is that she pronounced my surname correctly – although it is not a difficult one, it has proven more challenging for some over the years than I would have thought! Sam had asked me to come down to his office near the site designated for the Globe to have lunch and discuss the project. I went down to meet Sam shortly thereafter in the leaky, draughty building in Bear Gardens, which now houses the Education and Rehearsal Centre. On this visit, I also met the brilliant Patrick Spottiswoode, who served as our venerable director of Education from the outset until 2020. I literally broke bread – yes, a sandwich – with Sam at Bear Gardens and he showed me a miniature model of the Globe and gave me a guided tour of the site. He appeared to be convinced that I could be helpful – I wasn't so sure. Sam was known for collecting people!

When I arrived, some harsh realities were beginning to set in. Late in 1989, Sam learned that he had cancer. His colleagues knew nothing until the last few weeks of his life, and I'm told that he said nothing to his family until 1992. This is when practicality started. The price tag of the all-or-nothing complex that Sam ideally wanted to create was £24 million. Sam eventually saw sense in the suggestion that some of his advisers were making, which was to break the project into component parts, cost it accordingly and build the complex in digestible sections over time. With a more achievable figure of £8 million to raise for the concrete piazza on which the Globe would stand and the Globe itself, Sam's approach was that now people could see the building was underway, funds would follow.[19]

Globe Theatre interior. Courtesy of Shakespeare's Globe Photographer: Clive Sherlock

To realise Sam's vision of the Globe campus, we had to keep building after his death in 1993. The three-legged stool of theatre, education and exhibition all needed investment. Fundraising was critical to our future. One of the first things I did to show my commitment was to try to enthuse all my friends and colleagues to support this great idea which, for those who worked in the City, was literally across the bridge. An early fundraiser that I recall helping to organise was the Hop Ball at the Hop Exchange, which had served as the centre for hop trading for the brewing industry. Over the years, I served on an advisory committee shortly after I met Sam, several development committees and various capital campaigns. These became increasingly successful once we discovered who actually was interested in Shakespeare – more difficult than you might imagine at the time. In the early days, support from within the United Kingdom had been limited. There were some who thought we weren't needed, given that the Royal Shakespeare Company at Stratford already existed. The Globe was referred to disparagingly by some as just a replica; Disney was mentioned! Fortunately, the Globe had international support at the time, which remains important; as does the robust UK support that we now enjoy. Another key factor was the pivotal role played by Mark Rylance, our first artistic director, who with his theatrical

Mark Rylance as Olivia in Twelfth Night at Shakespeare's Globe Courtesy of Shakespeare's Globe. Photographer: John Tramper

genius brought our artistic merits to the world's attention. One of his brilliant performances that I still recall vividly was when in 2012 he returned to the Globe and played Olivia in *Twelfth Night* opposite Stephen Fry's Malvolio.

Fundraising continued apace. We raised £7.5 million for the building of the Education and Rehearsal Studios in 2010 and £7.5 million for the completion of the Sam Wanamaker Playhouse, our candlelit indoor Jacobean theatre, in January 2014. With the completion of the Playhouse, the Globe campus became operational throughout the year. As a member of the board for 12 years, including serving as deputy chair, I had the privilege of being part of a very exciting and rewarding journey as our strategy developed and our operations grew. With Neil Constable as our energetic, thoughtful and ambitious CEO, we were fortunate to have a strong executive team. As we developed our brand proposition and scaled our operations, we grew into a respected, much-admired global brand, recognised for performance, scholarship and new writing. But we never forgot our origins and the struggle it had taken to get to this point. It is noteworthy that we are almost unique among London's cultural institutions in that we did not receive government subsidy prior to the pandemic. We always tried to cut our cloth accordingly. This pre-pandemic lack of government funding gave us greater flexibility and control over our destiny. The board was always prudent and the Globe therefore had significant reserves on the balance sheet as a cushion. However, no one was prepared for the extent of the shutdown which the pandemic necessitated. Things changed fast and we have reshaped our business plan to reflect a smaller business in the near term, but very much with the aim of growing again over time. Sam's independent spirit and relentless energy live on at the Globe.

What has particular resonance with me is how we drove the development of our international ambition and relationships. We historically had strong relationships in the Old Commonwealth, including Canada and New Zealand, from Sam's time. However, the Cultural Olympiad in 2012 ahead of the London Olympic Games was our international accelerator. It brought 37 international theatre companies from 37 countries to our stage – each performed a Shakespeare play in their native language and the audience for each performance comprised members of their own extended community, underlining the diversity of London's population. These companies have continued to use the Globe as a point of reference and we have built close linkages with some of them. When I was visiting Dhaka, I was invited to watch Dhaka Theatre rehearsing its Bangla language version of *The Tempest*. I was asked by the director if there was too much music and dance in their approach for the

Globe. I said, "Don't change a thing – it will work brilliantly on our stage" – and so it did. The Afghan Company, by contrast, was unable to rehearse safely in Kabul and we had to raise extra funds to subsidise secure rehearsals in Paris.

Another inspired international moment occurred in 2013, when our then artistic director, Dominic Dromgoole, presented the board with his idea for a two-year world tour of *Hamlet*, covering 200 countries. As a trustee had to consider risk and reputation very carefully, my mind first turned to health and safety, budgets and visa requirements – how many passports would each actor need? And what about the production's carbon footprint? However, the board was gradually won over by the inspired idea of building bridges with communities around the world, and this we did valiantly. Only North Korea proved impregnable; and while Syria was out of bounds, we managed to address this by playing in the refugee camps in Jordan and Calais. We played in five cities in mainland China, where there is huge appetite for our content. Many people don't realise that Shakespeare was first translated into Mandarin over 100 years ago. This tour of a dozen intrepid young actors came back to London uneventfully, with their final overseas performance fittingly at Elsinore in Denmark in the presence of the Queen of Denmark, which my wife and I attended on a chilly Copenhagen evening. At this time, the Globe also started using digital technologies to reinforce this burgeoning international footprint, through Globe on Screen and Globe Player – a theatre first which took our work and more than 60 films direct to a wide variety of audiences, many aged under 35, in 180 countries. Digital has, of course, become integral to everything we do today at the Globe, recognising that social distancing and physical capacity limits will need to be complemented by live streaming of performances and digital outreach and interactivity for Globe Education.

As the current chair of Shakespeare's Globe Council, I retain a close relationship with the Globe today. The Globe is still a young organisation, not quite 21; and while our resilience has been tested through this very difficult period, along with the whole creative arts community in the United Kingdom, we have reflected and will rebuild. The Globe has a clear purpose known as our cause which will continue to guide us.

5. Conclusion

You will know when you have found your purpose because it will energise you; it will give you joy; you will never feel you've done enough; it will frame your overall thinking; it will inform your behaviours. It will excite you; you will want to share your enthusiasm and engage others you know. When you come across inevitable roadblocks, you will not be easily deterred – you will be resilient. You will be at your most resourceful to find an appropriate circumvention route. You will invest, nurture, protect and challenge. You will argue your case increasingly well. You will be relentless. So I encourage you to get going or continue on your purposeful journey. There is so much to be done – whether it's local community volunteering or something more transformative. Make some choices which are right for you. Play your part. Remember the words of William Shakespeare, who wrote so aptly on purpose in *As You Like It*. As Jacques declaims in Act 2: "All the world's a stage, and all the men and women merely players. They have their exits and their entrances; And one man (or woman) in his (her) time plays many parts. His (her) acts being seven ages."[20] This is the age of the rising next generation.

Notes

1 James E Hughes, Susan E Massenzio and Keith Whitaker, *The Voice of the Rising Generation: Family Wealth and Wisdom* (Bloomberg/John Wiley, 2014).
2 "Dame Polly Courtice's perspective on the sustainability agenda for businesses in the Covid-19 landscape and beyond – Time for a Rethink", Ispahani Advisory Webinar series (June 2020).
3 Founded in 1863, the ICRC is an independent, neutral humanitarian organisation working to help people affected by armed conflict and violence in 90 countries. ICRC, "We're all in this together Covid-19 a global crisis requiring a global response" (2021).
4 Mark Carney is the UN's special envoy on climate action and finance and is the author of *Value(s): Building a Better World for All* (William Collins, 2021).
5 Robert Mardini, "When rain turns to dust: Understanding and responding to the combined impact of armed conflicts and the climate and environment crisis on people's lives" (International Committee of the Red Cross, 2020).
6 University of Notre Dame Global Adaptation Initiative (ND-Gain) Country Index, Vulnerability rankings, 2018, https://gain.nd.edu/our-work/country-index/rankings/.
7 An initiative that aims to prepare young people to become productive citizens by connecting secondary-age education and training to employment and entrepreneurship.
8 Simon Sinek, *Start With Why: How Great Leaders Inspire Everyone to Take Action* (Penguin, 2011).
9 See Jed Emerson's chapter, "The purpose of capital: exploring our relationship with money and meaning", in this Special Report.
10 Charles Keidan, "Interview: James Chen", *Alliance* (4 December 2018), www.alliancemagazine.org/interview/interview-james-chen-2/.
11 www.britannica.com/biography/Mahatma-Gandhi.
12 See Jessica McGawley's chapter, "Effective mentorship for the next generation", in this Special Report.
13 James E Hughes, Susan E Massenzio and Keith Whitaker (n 1).
14 Alex Haley, *Roots* (Vintage Books, 1994). Quote sourced from www.goodreads.com/quotes/32907-in-every-conceivable-manner-the-family-is-link-to-our.
15 Vision Atlas, "Number of people affected by vision loss 2020", International Agency for the Prevention of Blindness (2020), http://atlas.iapb.org/global-burden-vision-impairment/.
16 PricewaterhouseCoopers and The Fred Hollows Foundation, "Investing in Vision: The Costs & Benefits of Ending Avoidable Blindness", www.hollows.org/Upload/FHFV3/Media/au/pdf/Other%20file%20downloads/PwC-Investing-in-Vision-Summary-Brochure_1.pdf.
17 A Visionary Partnership, "15 Years of Seeing is Believing", Standard Chartered and the International Agency for the Prevention of Blindness (2018), https://av.sc.com/corp-en/content/docs/A-partnership-vision-15-years-of-Seeing-is-Believing.pdf.
18 Diana Devlin, *Sam Wanamaker: A Global Performer* (Bloomsbury Publishing Plc, 2019).
Diana Devlin and Iraj Ispahani Wycombe Abbey School Speech, Headmistress's lecture, 2016.
19 Barry Day, *This Wooden 'O': Shakespeare's Globe Reborn* (Oberon Books in association with The Shakespeare Globe Trust, 1996).
20 William Shakespeare, *As You Like It*, Act 2, Scene 7.

II. Effective mentoring for the next generation

Jessica McGawley
Dallington Associates

To understand the [person], you have to know what was happening in the world when [they were] twenty.
– Napoleon Bonaparte[1]

1. Introduction

To understand any generation, we must understand what was happening in the world as they grew up. Until we do, we cannot fully grasp our own roles – as parents, advisers, mentors – in supporting them.

Like every generation, 16 to 24-year-olds today – those whom we refer to as Generation Z[2] – differ greatly from their parents and grandparents. They are a generation that have grown up in an era of fast and accessible information; self-directed learning; globalisation; human rights awareness; social media; the visible threat of climate change; fake news; and, most recently, the global COVID-19 pandemic. By and large, they are a socially conscious, inclusive, pragmatic and analytical generation. They are also a generation that like to communicate audio-visually – through images, videos, infographics and voice files.

GENERATION Z

SOCIALLY CONSCIOUS

Gen Z are the most racially diverse, liberal and tolerant generation in history. Gen Zs genuinely value a company's social impact and care strongly about the environment.

EDUCATED

50% of Gen Zs have attended college or university. They proactively seek learning opportunities such as internships and are keener to 'learn before they earn' than their Millennial predecessors.

TECH NATIVES

They are masters of social media, use up to 5 digital devices at one time, and are known as the app generation.

IMPATIENT

Their attention spans are on average 8 seconds, which is 4 shorter than Millennials. They thrive on instant gratification.

26% ARE ANXIOUS

26% of Gen Z suffer from anxiety, as compared to 21% of Millennials, 17% of Gen Xers and 9% of Boomers

PRAGMATIC

Gen Z have grown up during a global financial crisis and a pandemic. They are cautious with money (57% would choose saving over spending) and want both emotional and financial stability.

Unlike their tech immigrant parents, the tech natives of Generation Z have never known a world without the Internet and digital technology. Used to having a vast amount of information at their fingertips, they are set to become the most educated generation in history. Understandably, this is also a generation in which many experience feelings of anxiety.

Mentoring young people during these crucial developmental years can significantly improve outcomes for them, equipping them with the knowledge, tools and mechanisms to navigate life and evolve into self-aware, resilient people. In some circumstances, mentoring at this stage can offset the risk or the need for future, and potentially more public, intervention.

This is an age at which young adults are reluctant to openly communicate on certain subjects – and sometimes any subjects – with their parents. It is not unusual for there to be a change in the way that parents and children communicate at this age. However, it can be very difficult for a young person to find an alternative and trusted source from whom to seek the information and guidance that they need. For parents, it can be a particularly challenging time, in which many find themselves second guessing their children and, as a result, being unsure as to what support to offer or what boundaries to set. If you are very close to something or spend too long staring at it, it can be hard to see the solution and – with the best intentions in the world – you risk over-compensating. Although motivated by love and a desire to help, the efforts of parents can sometimes hinder rather than help development at this age.

The generational gap between today's 16 to 24-year-olds and their parents, advisers and employers can be hard to bridge; but this can be made easier. Having someone who can help bridge the gap – someone whom a developing adult can relate to, can ask awkward questions of and can call on in situations of extreme anxiety – can be hugely helpful. In this capacity, a mentor can make all the difference, helping to preserve existing relationships and supporting developing adults in becoming the best versions of themselves.

Mentoring at any age or stage is valuable; although, as with most things, starting young helps to establish a solid foundation to build on. Just as there are no teachers who have not been students, most mentors have themselves been a mentee at some point. The younger we learn, the more we can benefit and the sooner we can pass on our experience. By starting this process earlier in life, the rising next generation can better manage the emotional aspects of succession and, in turn, pass these on to the next generation when it is time.

In this chapter, we look at the particular circumstances facing children of affluence and explore how mentoring can help to develop and prepare them for a life contextualised by wealth, helping them to achieve their goals, develop resilience and autonomy, and become the most fulfilled, capable versions of themselves that they can.

2. Choice, anxiety and the importance of failure

Day by day, what you choose, what you think and what you do is who you become.
– Heraclitus[3]

People today face more choices every day than any preceding generation: from the coffee they drink in the morning to the eco-friendly water bottle they accessorise with, and from the college courses they embark on to the career paths they follow. For children of affluence, the plethora of choices and opportunities are even more diverse, which can be both liberating and sometimes crippling. With so much possibility within reach, how can a young and inexperienced person know that they are making the right, if not the best possible, choices?

Choice brings with it responsibility and, in turn, a pressure to succeed. Although it can feel like it, choice does not equate to control. The trap that many young people from affluent backgrounds fall into is believing that because they have choice, they must succeed; and because they have such a clear advantage, everything must be perfect. Pleasing parents is frequently of paramount emotional importance and failure to achieve perfection is often felt not only as failure in the moment, but also as an indication of failure as a person.

Experiences such as these trigger anxiety and impact confidence. Expressions of anxiety and depression can be perceived as attention seeking if not understood. Left undiagnosed, chronic anxiety can deeply affect an individual's health in the long term. Fear of failure prevents us from being able to make decisions and ultimately from assuming responsibility for, and taking control of, our own lives. But we can choose to frame our view on this differently. We can choose to see our failures as lessons rather than as the object of shame and embarrassment.

Ninety per cent of adults are immune to chickenpox because they had it when they were children. Parents don't tend to protect their children from catching chicken pox, because we know that it is safer for a child to build future immunity by catching the virus than it is to shield them from it and have them catch it as adults, when the risks are greater. The same thinking can and should be applied to failure. By shielding your child from failure, you prevent them from learning

"Choice brings with it responsibility and, in turn, a pressure to succeed. Although it can feel like it, choice does not equate to control."

valuable lessons, building resilience and developing self-esteem. If a person is to become independent, they need to know it's okay to fall down, because it is only by falling down and getting back up again that we learn to walk.

3. The importance of individuation to finding purpose
'Individuation' – a term attributed to Swiss psychiatrist and psychoanalyst Carl Gustav Jung[4] – describes the process of self-realisation: the discovery and experience of meaning and purpose through which one develops their personal identity and becomes who they are. This process can last a lifetime, but can feel at its most intense during the mid to late adolescent years from 16 to 24. These are the years in which we typically forge our identity and enter adulthood. For many of us, the experiences we have, the influences we encounter and the relationships we form during this time are those that we carry into our adult lives and, for better or worse, that impact on our individuation.

Individuation is a process of self-discovery made possible by a shift from the unconscious to the conscious mind. It allows us to see ourselves and to change what we can and accept what we can't. Individuation in itself is not typically a conscious choice, but something that happens to us all, to varying degrees, as we are exposed to the opportunities and challenges of life. These experiences test our boundaries and force us to acknowledge parts of ourselves that we didn't know existed.

If the individuation process stagnates and does not complete (perhaps due to trauma, harmful family dynamics or mental health challenges), a person can become depressed, anxious and overly dependent on others. When our sense of self is shaken, everything can feel like a challenge and anything but praise a criticism. This can often lead to questionable choices, particularly when forming new friendships and romantic or professional relationships, as we seek emotional reinforcement in the wrong places.

If we choose to approach the process of individuation more consciously, with curiosity and a commitment to self-understanding without judgement, then we can truly benefit from it. Doing so can also help to identify our sense of purpose. There are, of course, the lucky few who seem to have been born with an innate sense of purpose – a calling that has determined the course of their lives from a young age. For the vast majority, though, locating purpose is a more involved process and one that demands application. To add to the challenge, purpose can change more than once within a lifetime – for example, when a person becomes a parent. We continue to change and evolve throughout our lifetimes, which is why individuation is a lifelong process.

A mentor acts as a guide on this journey, helping a mentee to realise their personal identity and develop self-esteem, self-awareness and self-reliance. In doing so, we develop independence and autonomy, which is an extremely important part of becoming who we are and standing on our own two feet.

4. Wellbeing is about balance

Like so many lasting concepts, it is the ancient Greeks that we have to thank for the concept of mentoring. When Odysseus left home to fight in the Trojan War and complete his 10-year odyssey thereafter, he entrusted his son to the care of his good friend, Mentor. The results of Mentor's counsel and guidance were so fruitful that his efforts have been remembered throughout history.

Definitions of 'mentoring' have evolved over time, with different models emerging to suit myriad contexts; but one thing they all have in common is the idea of a provider of counsel and guidance to someone less experienced. Something more than a teacher, but without the emotional involvement of a parent.

More often than not, mentoring practice is based on intergenerational counsel and guidance. It makes sense that the older, more experienced

MENTORSHIP

QUALITIES OF A MENTOR

EXPERIENCE BASED

Their guidance and approach will often stem from their own knowledge and experiences.

ACTIVE LISTENER

They are someone who hears both verbal and non-verbal communication and helps the mentee clarify their thoughts.

ENCOURAGING

They encourage mentees in pursuit of their goals, sharing inspirational material and experiences. They are supportive through challenges and perceived failures.

EMPATHETIC

They are able to experience their mentee's thoughts and feelings from their point of view, rather than from their own.

AUTHENTIC

A mentor works in a way that is unique to them and not from a handbook.

A GOOD MENTOR...

BUILDS TRUST

It is about developing a relationship based on trust and bonding. Unlike in therapy or coaching, a mentor will share their experiences including mistakes and failures as they often contain lessons.

STAYS OPEN

A mentee should feel that nothing is inappropriate or off the table to discuss with their mentor.

HOLDS YOU ACCOUNTABLE

The relationship may entail setting goals, clarifying or realigning them, and regularly reviewing the mentee's actions towards these.

LEARNS WITH YOU

The mentor helps the mentee to learn and develop, be that in communication, leadership, knowledge or life skills. This learning is often reciprocal.

PROMOTES INDEPENDENCE

The purpose of mentoring is to get the mentee to a place where they feel confident in their own abilities and no longer need the support.

A MENTOR IS NOT...

AUTHORITATIVE

A mentor will not expect you to learn vicariously through their experience, or tell you what you should or should not do.

JUDGEMENTAL

A mentor will not condemn you for your mistakes, thoughts or views. They will approach these with curiosity and understanding.

A THERAPIST

While a mentor is supportive and trustworthy, they do not work therapeutically or replace the need for psychological support.

A FIXER

One of the mentor's key roles is to help the mentee know themselves. If the mentor falls into the trap of 'fixing', this opportunity for learning is removed.

person should guide the younger, less experienced. We have found that developing adults relate better to mentors who are older than them, but younger than their parents. As a general rule, we match mentees with mentors who are in the region of 10 to 15 years older than themselves. Something else that is very important in a mentoring relationship is reciprocity. The mentoring relationship does not flow in a single direction, as does the relationship between teacher and student. The mentor and mentee learn from each other simultaneously. In this way, the mentor learns from the experiences of the mentee, preventing them from forming assumptions based on their own experience, keeping their understanding of context current and constantly renewing their abilities and credentials as mentors. There is no one-size-fits-all solution in mentoring, so a mentor must learn from their mentees if they are to successfully mentor each and every one of them.

A successful mentoring journey guides an individual towards establishing personal identity and resilience through the development of self-awareness and independence. Abraham Maslow developed a motivational theory based on the fundamentals of human need and how this relates to personal fulfilment.[5] Maslow ranks these needs in a five-tier hierarchy, culminating in human fulfilment. On the bottom

"A successful mentoring journey guides an individual towards establishing personal identity and resilience through the development of self-awareness and independence."

STAGES OF MENTORSHIP

1. BUILDING

Strong foundations are important, so the first thing the mentor and mentee do is get to know each other by discussing interests, sharing experiences and dreams, establishing boundaries and building trust.

2. GOAL SETTING

Sometimes we appropriate the goals of others as our own without realising. Identifying and setting your own goals, and not those of your parents, peers or mentors, is paramount.

3. DEVELOPMENT

This is about achieving goals, drawing on a combination of practical and emotional support. The guidance, tools and support shared help mentees navigate new experiences and events in their lives.

4. REFLECTION

As we develop, the goalposts can often move. Sometimes a plan must be adapted to meet changing needs. It is important to regularly review and realign the development plan, ensuring it places emphasis on the right areas at any given point in the mentoring journey.

5. GRADUATION

Knowing when to let go is important, but doing it too soon can be counterintuitive. A parent always hovers behind their child, arms outstretched, when the training wheels are removed from their first bicycle, just until they are sure the child is steady and can ride alone. A graduated phase-out of the mentoring relationship helps ease the transition to full independence.

rung of the hierarchy sit physiological needs, followed by security, belonging, esteem and, at the pinnacle, self-actualisation – the point at which we become fulfilled beings.

At Dallington Associates, we take a more cyclical approach to needs-based human development and fulfilment, using a model based on the interdependent and interrelational factors of cognitive, emotional, social and physical development. We believe all of these factors to be important, but also recognise that for every mentee, that which takes precedence in any one moment will change over time, influenced by personal development, as well as by outside factors affecting their lives.

5. The wheel of wellbeing

The quadrants in the figure opposite represent the four aspects of development that constitute a person's wellbeing. For a developing adult, all four aspects are significant. It is important to understand that a lag in one area will have an impact on all other areas. Wellbeing is about balance. If a young person – let's call her Lucy – stops exercising and eating properly, she will stop sleeping well, which will affect her cognitive development and ability to study effectively. She will become moody, which will have implications for her social interactions and

"We take a more cyclical approach to needs-based human development and fulfilment, using a model based on the interdependent and interrelational factors of cognitive, emotional, social and physical development."

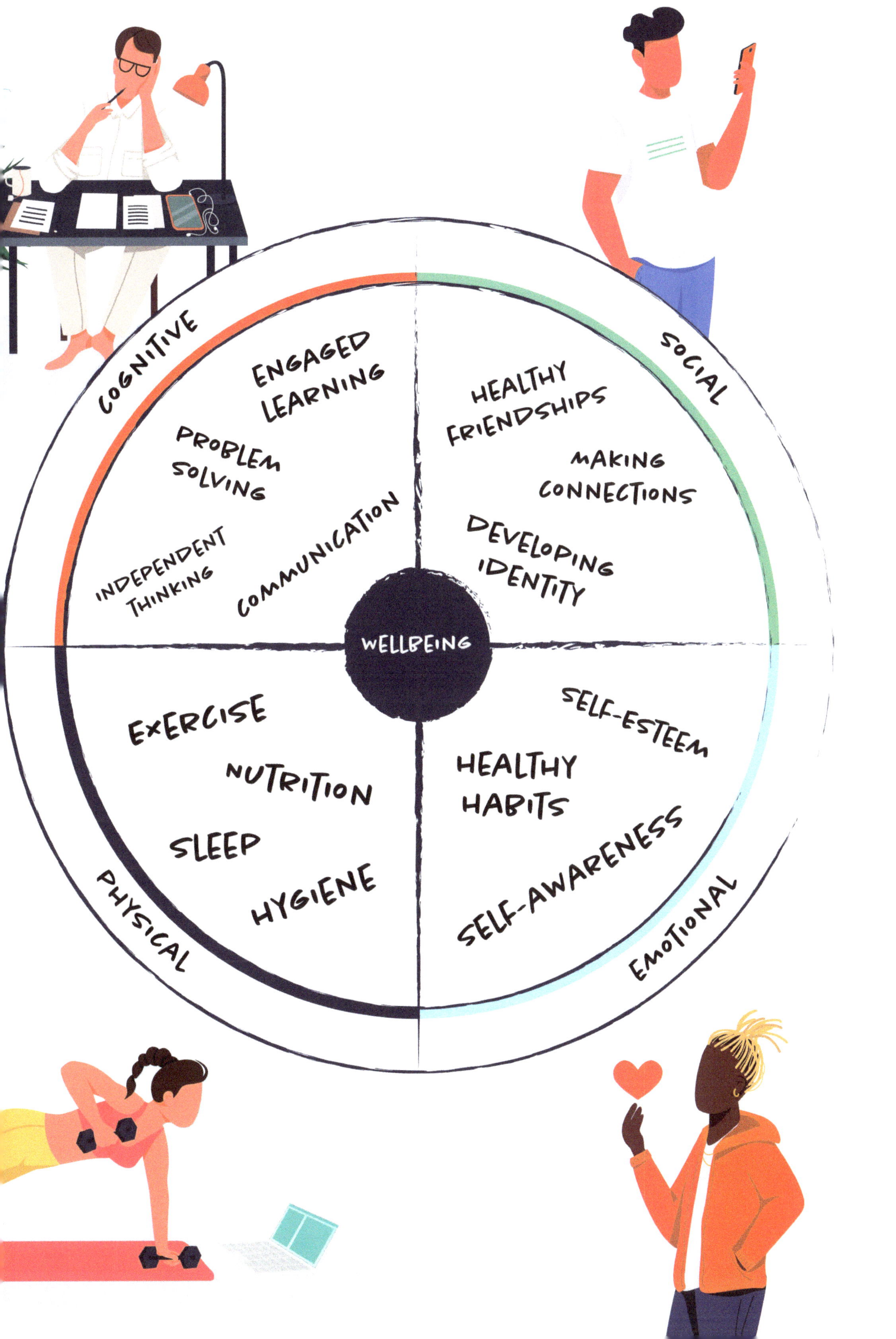

COGNITIVE
ENGAGED LEARNING
PROBLEM SOLVING
INDEPENDENT THINKING
COMMUNICATION
SOCIAL
HEALTHY FRIENDSHIPS
MAKING CONNECTIONS
DEVELOPING IDENTITY
WELLBEING
PHYSICAL
EXERCISE
NUTRITION
SLEEP
HYGIENE
EMOTIONAL
SELF-ESTEEM
HEALTHY HABITS
SELF-AWARENESS

relationships; and this in turn can impact on her mental health. Assessing Lucy's behaviour and progress through the four lenses of cognitive, social, physical and mental wellbeing helps to build a picture of where she is struggling most, which forms the basis of a plan for improvement. What would be even better, though, is if Lucy were able to self-identify her deterioration and form her own plan for improvement.

6. A personalised wheel of wellbeing

Exploring the root cause of Lucy's changing needs helps both Lucy and her mentor to reach a more in-depth understanding of what is going on, based on the interrelational nature of the four quadrants. For example, Lucy may already have been struggling with certain aspects of her life for a while. She is shy and finds it hard to make new friends. She is becoming increasingly paranoid that nobody likes her and that people are talking behind her back. Her self-esteem is very low, so she stops caring for herself. Her diet deteriorates, as do her sleep patterns. The exhaustion and paranoia are affecting her mental health. Lucy creates her personal wheel of wellbeing, as in the figure opposite. The wheel is filled with all of the things that Lucy wants to do in order to lead a more balanced life. By keeping track of her own performance in each of the four quadrants, Lucy can recognise that her mental health is suffering (because she has stopped completing the activities in her social and emotional quadrants), and can ask for help before someone else needs to intervene. Lucy can then update her wheel to reflect her new needs. In this way, the wheel gives Lucy greater control of her own wellbeing. Her ability to identify the issue and be a part of the solution is empowering.

In practical terms, what this means is that to effectively mentor a developing adult, we need to look at the whole person through these four lenses, working with individuals to assess areas for improvement and formulating personal development plans based on these assessments. These plans are not finite. As an individual progresses through the mentoring journey, the balance can shift and the plan may need revising. Some mentees include additional dimensions in their wellbeing plans – for instance, spiritual wellbeing. Certain aspects may need revisiting as dynamics shift. The wheel is not so much cyclical as inter-dimensional and, in hindsight, would possibly be better represented by a three-dimensional model.

7. Boundaries are friends, not foes

Psychologist Erik Erikson's theory of psychosocial development identifies eight stages of development throughout a human being's life.[6] The stages to which he equates the developing adult (spanning adolescence and young adulthood) are those of identity versus role confusion and intimacy versus isolation.

LUCY'S WELLBEING
COGNITIVE
READING TIME
INTENTION SETTING
MORNING STUDY TIME
EXERCISE CREATIVITY
SOCIAL
AUTHENTIC CONNECTIONS
VOLUNTEER @RSPCA
BALANCE TIME SPENT ONLINE
JOIN A SOCIETY AT UNI
EMOTIONAL
REMEMBER H-A-L-T BEFORE REACTING
SPEAK UP WHEN FEELING OVERLOOKED
WRITE IN MY DAILY JOURNAL
FOLLOW MORE AUTHENTIC INFLUENCERS
PHYSICAL
DRINK MORE WATER
PHONE OFF BY 11PM
HOT YOGA 2x A WEEK
DAILY WALK

The formation of identity is a prominent and often challenging theme during teenage-hood and a person's early 20s. For developing adults from affluent backgrounds, and especially for those studying and living abroad, it can be a particularly confusing and often isolating experience. In your earlier years, personal identity is largely tied to family and place. Away from both of these, life can seem complicated. In later years, identity becomes increasingly linked to purpose. Inherited wealth can make it harder for a person to locate their sense of purpose, frequently resulting in feelings of low self-esteem.

Having the freedom to explore one's identity is exciting; but to do so without boundaries or guidance can be overwhelming. Establishing boundaries helps us to feel more secure. Learning the difference between right and wrong, what is acceptable behaviour and what is not, is an essential part of every person's moral and social development. After all, if you're going to choose to break a rule, you've got to know what the rule is. Boundaries help us to make choices that are in our own interest and that do not make us or others vulnerable. Without boundaries, we have no guide, no benchmark; and this can trigger alarming feelings of chronic anxiety.

If you observed a rollercoaster attendant lowering a safety bar for other passengers to keep them safely in their seats and then noticed that they hadn't lowered your own bar, you would ask them to do so or would do so yourself. In this case, the attendant has demonstrated a boundary that you were not previously aware of. Now that you have seen the bar and understand its benefit, you naturally want yours lowered too. If you didn't know that the bar existed, you might ride without it, putting yourself and your companions at great risk. You wouldn't be having fun. You would be vulnerable. Boundaries, by their very nature, encourage a direction of travel towards self-improvement and, until we learn to establish them for ourselves, must be learned from our parents and our teachers, our employers and rollercoaster attendants.

As a developing adult, the testing of boundaries is an important part of the process of individuation. It is a natural instinct to do so. This behaviour is frequently read as dissatisfaction and unhappiness. A parent's natural response is often to acquiesce and even to overcompensate, but this can lead to unrealistic expectations. The world and the people in it will not always bend to someone's will. Giving in to someone's whims and making things easier than they would normally be is setting them up for disappointment. Fast, effortless material gain rarely equates to long-term benefit.

As a parent, learning to say no – or at the very least, delaying gratification – is as important, if not more so, for children as it is for parents. Delayed gratification is an important socialising concept. By choosing to wait for something, saving up for it, working towards it, we understand its value. The realisation that something that is desired is not needed immediately, that without it the world will not fall apart, and that the sense of reward is greater when we do finally receive something or achieve a goal is an important lesson. It teaches a person the difference between need and want, which helps us to master self-discipline and to grasp the true value of things. Delayed gratification also helps a person to develop a richer, more creative internal world, because by not having every desire met with immediacy, they are forced to turn to themselves for satisfaction, distraction and fulfilment.

As we mature, we learn to set our own boundaries for ourselves and for others, creating the space that we need to be able to achieve the things that we need to achieve in the way that we choose to achieve them. This is an important part of forming and maintaining both platonic and romantic relationships.

The next developmental stage in Erik Erikson's theory is that of generativity versus stagnation, addressing the years from 40 to 65, when many of us are parents and most of us are consumed with the

"The world and the people in it will not always bend to someone's will. Giving in to someone's whims and making things easier than they would normally be is setting them up for disappointment."

question of how to make our mark on the world. As we have already explored earlier in the chapter, the process of individuation and the finding of purpose are not finite goals. As we grow and evolve, so do our circumstances and so do our goals and purpose. For this reason, the mentoring relationship at any stage in life must also adapt to keep pace and remain relevant.

8. Independence and autonomy through learned behaviours
Life away from home for the first time holds many adventures, but also many potential pitfalls. Wealthy families often have staff and for a developing adult – let's call him Anil – his arrival at university may be the first time that he has had to think about carrying out certain daily tasks. Anil's family has a driver, a personal assistant, a cook and a cleaner, a housekeeper and security guards. Before he arrived at university, Anil never had to do the grocery shopping, cook his meals, drive himself to appointments or clean his flat. It isn't that Anil can't do these things, but that he hasn't previously had to think about them – and they are time-consuming activities. Doing all these things while staying on top of his studies, keeping track of his day-to-day appointments, exercising regularly and making new friends is challenging. There just isn't enough time in the day. When things get a bit much, Anil is prone to losing things such as his keys, passport or headphones, which is frustrating and makes his life more complicated.

"The COVID-19 pandemic has forced many of us to reassess our work/life balance and reorganise our lives in order to remain safe and adhere to lockdown regulations."

Learning to stay on top of everything takes planning and organisation. There are tools and systems that can help Anil to manage his time and make sure that everything gets done. He doesn't have to be superman, but he does need to adopt some new behaviours.

One of the tools that Anil's mentor helps him to develop is his personalised schedule. This isn't just any schedule, but one informed by the four quadrants of the wheel of wellbeing. Each activity in the schedule is colour coded according to its quadrant. Different schedules will be heavier on some colours, weighted towards the areas in which Anil most needs to develop. Anil's daily action plan helps to build autonomy by helping him to meet his deadlines, take regular exercise, make friends and feel confident. By developing and reinforcing positive behaviours that will last a lifetime, he can learn to rely on himself, make his own choices and take responsibility for his own wellbeing.

These tools and behaviours don't just apply to university students, but are checks and balances that can be applied throughout a lifetime – particularly during periods of flux or trauma in which you might find yourself having to balance and cope with more than usual. As a recent example, the COVID-19 pandemic has forced many of us to reassess our work/life balance and reorganise our lives in order to remain safe and adhere to lockdown regulations. Most of us spread our lives across multiple physical environments on a regular basis – the office, gym, coffee shop, place of worship, club. The restrictions resulting from the pandemic have highlighted the extent to which our health, social and mental wellbeing, as well as our independence and autonomy, are linked to both the activities in which we engage and the environments in which we engage in them. Unable to adhere to our usual routines and behaviours, many of us have experienced misalignment and some depression. What is frustrating is that we can often see this happening, but feel powerless or lack the motivation to take action.

This is the moment at which the tools demonstrated by Lucy and Anil come into play. Using these mechanisms, we can take a step back and apply our four lenses of cognitive, social, physical and emotional wellbeing. Through these lenses, we can begin to understand how to prioritise, reorganise and reimagine a status quo. Using these tools, we can realign ourselves and maintain balance and productivity by developing new behaviours tailored to our new environments.

9. Empathy is empowering

One of the ways in which wealthier families often choose to teach their children about empathy is through philanthropic experience. These projects are beneficial to the communities they serve and are valuable vehicles for teaching a young person set to inherit significant wealth the importance of recognising and engaging with need in the wider world. However, these are often big projects, operating at scale. They don't always offer opportunities for personal engagement with the people they are helping and an opportunity to get to grips with their day-to-day struggles. Projects that involve immersing yourself in a community and walking a mile in other people's shoes are often abroad, and the context is thus far removed and 'other' in nature. It can be difficult for a young person to relate to these experiences and transfer the lessons when back in their own environment. In some sense, the lesson needs to be more literal, more relatable and more granular. One way to achieve this is to encourage young and developing adults to engage with charities or initiatives that are local to them and ideally of personal interest. Engaging in activities closer to home allows them to do more themselves and to directly engage with the people delivering support, as well as with the beneficiaries themselves. Face-to-face contact and the ability to see the results of their efforts first hand make it much easier to relate to the people they are helping, establish empathy and learn useful lessons that they can apply in their own lives.

Understanding value – whether financial or emotional – in relation to yourself or to others is an important part of developing empathy; and empathy is an essential aspect of successful relationships with friends and colleagues. Without empathy, we can have no view of how others experience things, making it incredibly difficult to relate to other people and for them to relate to us.

As well as a creator of opportunity and advantage, inherited wealth can be isolating. Many developing and young adults of affluence experience guilt about their privilege and making friends can sometimes be challenging. On the one hand, a person might feel guilty about the security and advantages afforded to them by wealth. This guilt can be exacerbated by the misplaced assumptions of some peers and colleagues that because they have money, they don't have real problems. It can be difficult to establish intimacy and form genuine attachments if you constantly feel like you have to apologise for your wealth and hide your true self for fear of being exposed to criticism or worse. On the other hand, a developing adult may find themselves in a situation in which they have many friends. In such a scenario, it can be hard to distinguish between genuine friendships and those that are far from genuine. This can make a person vulnerable. Trust is the basic foundation of any relationship. Without trust, genuine relationships cannot flourish.

10. We are who we choose to become

The only person you are destined to be is the person you decide to be.[7]
– Ralph Waldo Emerson

You cannot change the fact that you were born into wealth, but you can choose how you respond to circumstance. By investing time and effort in discovering who you are, overcoming your anxieties, seeking opportunities for improvement rather than perceiving failures and learning to make good decisions, you can create your own winning formula for life and be a better friend, family member, partner, leader and purposeful member of society.

Choosing to use your advantages for positive action rather than apologising for them can be both empowering and liberating. If life is a series of choices, every one of us has the power to choose to be the person that we want to be, starting with the decisions that we make every day. A good mentor helps a mentee to make choices; a great mentor helps to empower a mentee to make those choices independently.

Having themselves experienced the mentoring journey, many mentees become mentors later in life, passing on the wisdom that they have acquired to future generations. As a member of the rising next generation, the opportunity to be guided by someone who truly understands your context is invaluable. After all, who better to be guided by than someone who comes from a background that is not dissimilar; someone who understands the opportunities and pressures, has experienced the challenges and reaped the rewards; someone who is at once immersed and objective.

The mentoring experience is neither linear nor finite. The lessons learned along the way are lessons that can be applied and reapplied throughout a lifetime, whenever a person falls out of equilibrium and finds themselves in need of realignment. Nor does the learning simply flow in one direction. Just as the mentee is guided by the mentor, so must a mentor learn from the mentee. A mentor must always be learning so as to be constantly evolving and avoid stagnation. The world does not stand still: society, ideas and people evolve; and to be relevant and effective, counsel must be rooted in understanding.

Notes

1 Albert Manfred, *Napoleon Bonaparte* (Ediciones AKAL, 1988).
2 'Generation Z' refers to those born between 1995 and 2009. For the purpose of this chapter, we are referring to those within that generation aged 16 to 24.
3 Philip Wheelwright, *Heraclitus* (Colchis Books, 1974).
4 Carl Gustav Jung and Stanley M Dell, *The Integration of the Personality* (Routledge & K Paul, 1963).
5 Joseph E Gawel, Herzberg's *Theory Of Motivation And Maslow's Hierarchy Of Needs* (ERIC Clearinghouse on Assessment and Evaluation, 1997).
6 Patrick H Munley, "Erik Erikson's theory of psychosocial development and vocational behavior", 22(4) *Journal of Counseling Psychology*, pp314–319, 1975.
7 Ralph Waldo Emerson and Edward Waldo Emerson, *The Complete Works of Ralph Waldo Emerson* (AMS Press, 1979).

III. Safeguarding the family's digital narrative: how to navigate the challenges of the social media revolution

Charlie Bain
Digitalis

1. Introduction
For Abigail Disney – granddaughter and great-niece of Roy and Walt, who founded the Walt Disney Company – growing up in a family surrounded by untold riches was never entirely comfortable.

Deeply concerned about the remuneration of some of the lowest-paid staff at the company's theme park, Disneyland, she decided to take matters into her own hands and publicly shame the organisation that bears her name and made her extremely wealthy.

Using a combination of her Twitter account and a first-person article in the *Washington Post*, she criticised the $66 million annual pay of Disney's CEO and championed the rights of the employees working in Disney theme parks.[1] In July 2020, she took to Twitter again to criticise Walt Disney's decision to furlough thousands of low-paid workers during the COVID-19 pandemic after paying dividends to shareholders and bonuses to its executives.[2]

Just a few months earlier, in a different boardroom, Rupert Murdoch's 48-year-old son, James, was also taking his family to task. In a very public outburst, he strongly criticised his family's news outlets for downplaying the impact of the climate crisis.[3] It was a rare public attack by a company director on his own group's operations and shed light on the tensions and speculation over his 88-year-old father's succession plans.

What both these examples showed was the tension that often exists when members of very successful and high-profile families break away and cast doubt on their narratives. Both forging their own career paths, but indelibly linked to the family's heritage by name, Abigail Disney and James Murdoch were an intrinsic part of a family history, but their own values and personal views were at odds with the culture they grew up in.

Both made their declarations very publicly and deliberately. But often, such strident views aren't made so openly – especially with private families that don't run listed companies. On many occasions, a family might deal with this internally, but not want it aired to the world. However, what makes this hard is that, unlike 30 or even 20 years ago, we live in a multi-media age in which it is very hard to keep views and opinions private, however hard you try.

Today's rising next generation, groomed to take over the family business, have been brought up in the social media era and have really known nothing else. Often classed as Millennials or Generation Z, and

"Today's rising next generation, groomed to take over the family business, have been brought up in the social media era and have really known nothing else."

broadly born from 1981 onwards, they live in an era in which sharing, posting, liking, tweeting and commenting are all part of life. Inevitably, this has triggered a generational tension between how to preserve the family privacy while adapting to the digital revolution. One question that I am often asked, and which I see play out almost weekly in large families, is how to navigate this new world. What happens if the family's reputation – often built up over many years – is ruined in seconds by one rogue, ill-thought-through posting on the Internet?

What happens when a family name and business brand are synonymous, yet public postings on the Internet are discovered and business interests suffer value destruction as a result?

When does the family unit stop being about the 'We' and become the 'I'? And if you can't prevent that from happening, how can you take steps to make that private from the outside world?

This chapter doesn't attempt to address how to resolve intra-family conflict, but instead examines the critical area of digital privacy. We will look at the dizzying rise of social media and the digital world, and how this is used against some families and the rising next generation to ruin a reputation. We will examine how data collection from apps and 'digital footprints' might affect livelihoods; which new social media platforms to look out for; and the rise of fake news and deepfakes. And above all, we will provide advice and tips on how to traverse this tricky and constantly evolving landscape.

2. A family reputation

Most families that I have had the pleasure of advising are intensely private. Many have built up and passed on the family fortune quietly and beneath the radar. The matriarch and patriarch of the family are typically in their 60s, 70s or 80s (the Silent Generation and Boomers), and grew up in an era when keeping their counsel and not putting their heads above the parapet were the norm. Many do not run public companies, so are not bound to release information into the public domain. Generally, these families don't want a light shone on their business because there is no benefit. The 19th century essayist Walter Bagehot addressed this when talking about the British royal family. He argued that by remaining private to the public, the royals maintained their 'mystery', which is ultimately what the public liked about them.

"We must not let in daylight upon magic," he wrote in *The English Constitution* (1867).[4]

However, the digital revolution has made this hard, as remaining anonymous is impossible today. I always have to pinch myself when I am reminded that Facebook was only launched in its current guise in 2008; for some, it might feel like it's been around for a lot longer. Today, more than half (53%) of the world's population use social media.

The latest figures show that there are 4.2 billion social media users worldwide in 2021 – a 5% increase on a year ago. This is also 920 million more than the number of social media users in 2017, which represents a massive 32.2% jump in just five years. The average annual growth rate over this period is 7.2%.[5]

Figure 1. Global social media use

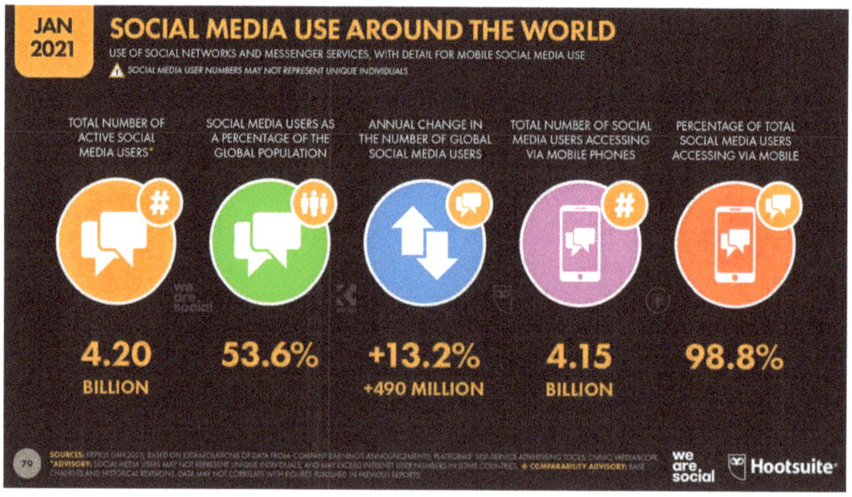

Source: DataReportal – Digital 2021: Global Overview Report

DataReportal's *Digital 2021: Global Overview Report*[6] highlights user figures for some of the most popular apps:

- Facebook – 2.7 billion users;
- Instagram – 1.2 billion users;
- TikTok – 689 million users; and
- Twitter – 353 million users.

According to Global Web Index, the average 16 to 24-year-old spends three hours and one minute on social media a day; while the average 25 to 34-year-old spends two hours and 37 minutes.[7] Compare that with 55 to 64-year-olds, where just 3% of the global population use social media – a figure which drops to around 2% of the over-65s.[8]

Facebook, Twitter and Instagram are now household names. TikTok – a relative newcomer in the social media revolution – is becoming incredibly popular with the under-25s and gaining users by the minute. LinkedIn now has more than 740 million users in 200 countries.[9]

Figure 2. Most-used social media platforms

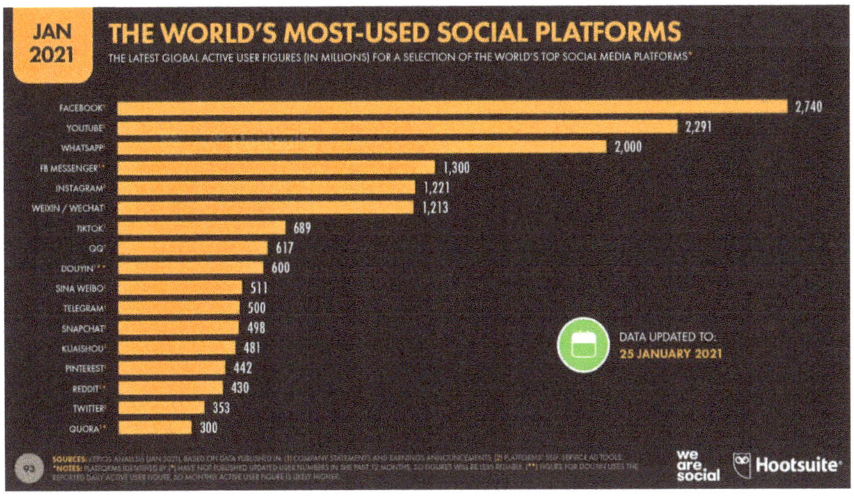

Source: DataReportal – Digital 2021: Global Overview Report

3. The hostile third party

Creating content for or sharing content on a platform has never been easier; and for many, the joy of seeing that content liked or shared is so great that thoughts of privacy go out the window. This feeling is not just limited to teenagers; those a lot older experience it too.

Many studies and articles have been written about the thrill of posting content and seeing the 'likes' or shares flood into your account. The dopamine rush that this generates in the brain is a crucial trigger in encouraging social media users to create content and post it online. And this is where the privacy and reputational aspects come into play.

Many clients that I advise often want to discuss the privacy issues around LinkedIn. LinkedIn, in theory, should be one of the more benign platforms when it comes to sharing content, because it is considered 'grown up' and just limited to business. However, for me, LinkedIn lures us into a false sense of security. Often, a person's entire education, work history, opinions and views are contained on this platform; and critically, their entire network is on show if the right privacy settings are not in place. Boundaries are blurred every day, with personal postings encroaching on the business stories. LinkedIn has also introduced new features that echo Instagram – such as LinkedIn Stories, which enables members and organisations to share images and short videos of their everyday professional moments.

Similar to Facebook, Twitter and Instagram, this 'digital library' of our lives is gold dust to someone with malintent. Whether a journalist, a hostile political activist, a disgruntled former employee of the family business – anybody who wants to cause the family harm can find a way to get hold of that content and highlight the poster and their family in a derogatory way.

One of the critical aspects of digital privacy invasion – which most people forget – is that it is often not the platform that you post on which causes the issue; it's the publication or outlet that spots it, finds the angle and repurposes the content into a damaging story or posting. Why, being part of the well-known family that you are a member of, is your posting a risk? Journalists, for instance, are experts in harvesting information online. If they want to write a derogatory story about a large family, they are likely to start poking around the matriarch or patriarch's digital footprint. Those family members from the Silent Generation are unlikely to have a significant digital presence. But their daughters, sons, grandsons, god daughters – you name it – may well have large digital footprints; and critically, these may contain information about the matriarch or patriarch. This second layer is frequently the weak link in a family trying to preserve a reputation.

The other point about content flying around online and being picked up by interested parties hell bent on causing trouble is that it's often very difficult to put the genie back in the bottle once it's out. I work with some of the best privacy lawyers in the world, who are experts at getting YouTube, Twitter, Facebook and the rest to remove content if it violates their terms or is defamatory. But often, this comes too late – the content has already been picked up and is hurtling around the Web at an alarming speed.

A really interesting example of this was a recent incident involving a documentary on the British royal family. In 1969, the queen agreed for the BBC to film a fly-on-the-wall documentary about the royal family. The 110-minute film was watched by 30 million people and remains one of the United Kingdom's most-viewed television broadcasts.

However, the queen decided that allowing the film to be broadcast was a bad idea and it never saw the light of day again. Since the early 1970s, it was kept under lock and key in an archive. That is, until January 2021, when an unknown user leaked it on YouTube. It was viewed thousands of times before Buckingham Palace and the BBC submitted a copyright claim and YouTube immediately took it down.[10] No real harm done, you might think; YouTube reacted quickly.

However, almost every newspaper globally reported on the leak and took the opportunity to dedicate acres of coverage to the contents of the documentary. It was followed up on blogs and a debate ensued as to who was responsible for leaking it. Some 50 years on, far from being private, it is literally all over the Internet.

4. The rising next generation and jobs

The rising next generation of a family, building their education and lives, should be acutely aware of the risk of content that is posted online either by them or about them coming back to haunt them in years to come. And as the royal family example shows, it need not be recent content; anyone with a grudge can surface content going back years online at any stage.

This not only has an effect on the wider family reputation, but could even cause issues when it comes to people in their 20s, 30s and 40s applying for a job – which in my view is worrying.

In research conducted by Career Builder, it was reported that 54% of employees have decided not to hire a candidate based on their social media profile. A staggering 70% of employers use social media to screen candidates.[11]

But what you post online can not only affect whether you get a job; it can also affect whether you are allowed to enter a country. Nearly all applicants for visas to work or study in the United States must submit their social media details under recently adopted rules. The State Department regulations require people to provide details of their social media accounts and five years' worth of email addresses and phone numbers.[12]

"The rising next generation of a family, building their education and lives, should be acutely aware of the risk of content that is posted online either by them or about them coming back to haunt them in years to come."

In August 2019, it was reported that an incoming Harvard freshman was blocked from entering the United States due to content on his social media pages. Even worse, the content that was deemed problematic was alleged to have come from his friends' activity, rather than his own.

5. How digitally private are the rising next generation?
But are Millennials and Generation Z really that bad when it comes to openly sharing data and social media? This is an interesting debate.

My own anecdotal evidence suggests that they are actually pretty good. When I used to conduct digital privacy audits on behalf of my family office clients five years ago, there would be a sea of open social media accounts with pictures, home addresses and comments, free for all to access. But I have seen a shift in this area, with the 20 to 40-year-old generation in particular becoming much more aware of their online privacy.

One US survey found that, across all age ranges, participants indicated that they do adjust privacy settings where possible. Notably, the team found that the large majority of participants adjust at least some of their account settings, although Millennials make more privacy adjustments on all of their accounts (67% of Millennials versus 50% of

"With the intricate details of our digital lives stored by these platforms, what happens if they fall into the wrong hands and are used inappropriately? What happens if there is a hack or a leak? It doesn't bear thinking about how the worst-case scenario could change lives."

Gen Z participants). Ironically, nearly 60% of Gen Zers – the generation known for having been brought up on technology – said that they had not received education about safety online.[13]

Anna-Sophie Harling is uniquely placed to comment on the rising next generation and privacy. As managing director for Europe at NewsGuard, an online service that rates and ranks news websites for reliability, she is also on the content board of Ofcom. Despite her extensive experience and expertise in all things digital, she is also – critically – under the age of 30.

Harling feels that Generation Z and Millennials are not necessarily that concerned about privacy when it comes to the frenetic need to use social media and share data. "By and large, users are concerned about privacy in the abstract," she told me. "But when it comes to making choices about what personal data to share, they make very little effort to properly read the terms and conditions. A good example is when it recently emerged there were data privacy concerns around WhatsApp; a lot of people instantly moved to Signal and Telegram. But a lot of people did that not because they were overly worried about the privacy of their data, but more because Elon Musk tweeted, 'Use Signal.'"

Sharing data, rather than simply placing it publicly online, is another risk that I am always highlighting to my clients. In October 2020, the House Judiciary Committee issued a report on its investigation of competition in the digital market. The committee found that Facebook, Apple, Google and Amazon have too much market power, and have used this power for anti-competitive purposes. The committee's view of the tech giants' behaviour is best reflected in the following scathing remark: "To put it simply, companies that once were scrappy, underdog startups that challenged the status quo have become the kinds of monopolies we last saw in the era of oil barons and railroad tycoons."[14]

One similarity of platforms such as Facebook, Twitter and Instagram, which many people didn't stop to think about in the early days, is that they are all free. And like many things that are free in life, there is a reason for this: we sign up without paying; they get our data.

For the rising next generation, this is a concern. Some Generation Zs, for instance, have never known a life in which they didn't hand over data to tech giants. With the intricate details of our digital lives stored by these platforms, what happens if they fall into the wrong hands and are used inappropriately? What happens if there is a hack or a leak? It doesn't bear thinking about how the worst-case scenario could change lives. The implications of a massive data leak could take years longer to clean up than an oil spill.

Harling is more confident on this front, believing that regulation and new instruments such as the General Data Protection Regulation and the right to be forgotten are just some of a number of measures that will give us more control over our data in the future.

"Regulation will definitely help in the future," she said. "Regulation could ensure, for example, that when you delete a Facebook or Instagram account, the data will be truly deleted."

6. Disinformation

The other aspect of the Internet that the rising next generation will have to learn to grapple with is how to decipher and navigate disinformation or avoid becoming the victim of it.

When Donald Trump popularised the phrase 'Fake News' in many of his broadcasts and broadsides, he was globalising an emerging phenomenon. Yet propaganda and disinformation are as old as politics itself; they have been around for centuries.

What was new about 'Fake News' was how it was disseminated by social media – driven by short soundbites and tantalising video clips. It preyed on the vulnerability of our short attention spans, especially those of the young. We are now bombarded by so much information that we prefer bite-sized bits of news and analysis, and are likely to digest sometimes hundreds of these a day. If a short video clip of a CEO, a politician or another high-profile person is sent to us, we are likely to view it if it's brief. We may immediately spot it as fake or a joke; but it will still sit in the memory. Or we may believe it. Before we know it, it becomes fact. That's why fake news is so insidious. It disorientates us.

Unsubstantiated and frankly false rumours are flourishing under the radar on the Internet every day, and most of them are easy to spot. However, others aren't, and sharing these rumours is now a major reputational vulnerability.

Let me explain why. The other day, I was called by a family whose son and heir was in his early 40s. One evening, tired after a long day working for the family business, he shared what he thought was an interesting story about how to avoid catching COVID-19 on his Facebook page and wrote a brief comment. The story, unbeknown to him, was in fact fake. Within minutes, the family's PR representative had received a call from the media asking why he was propagating a rumour which was actually a danger to public health. There was also concern from the family that if the story went live, the reputational fall-out would impact on the family's investments. Luckily, the story never appeared; but these are the kinds of extreme reputational issues that families must consider.

Celebrities and high-profile names who shared false rumours online linking 5G to the COVID-19 outbreak were labelled 'super-spreaders' and pilloried in the press. The bottom line is that you don't even need to create the content these days to become a story.

7. Deepfakes

There is a wonderful quote: "A lie can travel halfway around the world while the truth is putting on its shoes." This line perfectly exemplifies the lightning speed at which disinformation can travel in the social media age, before being proved entirely incorrect. With delicious irony, this is supposedly attributed to Mark Twain; yet there has been much debate online (yes, you guessed it) as to whether Twain actually said it or the attribution itself is a lie.

Deepfakes are also a deeply concerning internet phenomenon that the rising generation will have to grapple with in the future. A 'deepfake' is a synthetic video of a person generated by AI software. Except it's not that person – it's a fake. It can enable anyone to create false evidence of someone doing or saying something that they never did or said. A deepfake of a politician can be devastating, and can trigger untold chaos and unrest.

In March 2021, videos circulating online that purported to show Hollywood actor Tom Cruise practising his golf swing, performing a magic trick and telling an anecdote about former Soviet leader Mikhail Gorbachev were revealed as deepfakes. The highly realistic videos went viral across social media platforms, despite the actor having no involvement or even knowledge of the videos until they were released.

The visual effects specialist and creator of the deepfake Tom Cruise videos came forward to say that he wanted to make people aware of what they were watching, adding that the speed at which the technology is advancing could pose problems in the future.[15]

I would say that the word 'problem' is an understatement. This is a huge issue which we will have to address – and fairly rapidly. Synthetic media is on the increase because traditional video production is so unscalable. Why hire actors, a studio and producers when you can make a video using synthetic media for one-third of the cost and in one-tenth of the time?

Apply this to the family office or corporate world. Very soon, I'm convinced that a video of a company CEO addressing stakeholders will be synthetically made, rather than wasting their precious time filming it. Then consider the fact that such software can be used inappropriately. Fraudulent clips of that business leader could highlight a half-truth about the company which could send it out of business.

Fake videos of central bankers could send markets into freefall. Trusted news organisations might scramble to verify that a video is true and reveal whether it is or isn't; but often, by then it's too late. We live in a world where people react immediately.

A private family may have a video made about it and journalists may swarm to the family home to check whether the story is true. By the time they have confirmed it is *not* true, the very fact that the video has been made has become a story in itself. So a low-profile family which has done nothing to get news coverage may suddenly become the centre of scrutiny.

With Generation Z now becoming experts in home video making, we have a whole new stable of humans who can create content such as deepfakes very easily and very quickly. It won't be long before you will be able to access an app on your smartphone and send a deepfake live within minutes. Damian Collins, digital culture and sport select committee chairman in the United Kingdom, warned in February 2019 that deepfakes are "one of the most serious threats that democracy faces".[16] In March 2021, the US Federal Bureau of Investigation warned that they are the next major cyber threat.[17]

Rest assured: you will hear a lot more about deepfakes in the future.

8. The new apps on the block

Leaning quickly about new and emerging social media platforms and their privacy implications will also be critical for the rising next generation.

In the last year or so, we have seen the emergence of several alternative social media apps, such as Parler, Gab, Clubhouse, Rumble, MeWe, CloutHub and DLive. But what exactly are these newcomers and what new digital privacy concerns do they raise? With Facebook and Twitter increasingly banning accounts with far-right narratives, users are being driven to find other platforms in sometimes dark corners of the Internet. The increasing complexity and fragmentation of the online landscape are creating new digital risks, making it crucial to understand the unique political, legal and technical characteristics of each platform.

Clubhouse is an audio-based app that allows users listen to conversations in chatrooms, with an invitation model to attract new users. Any user can start a conversation in a 'private room'. But as I write, there are concerns that hostile third parties could infiltrate a chatroom, listen in, record the conversations and post them online.

"We have a whole new stable of humans who can create content such as deepfakes very easily and very quickly. It won't be long before you will be able to access an app on your smartphone and send a deepfake live within minutes."

9. Tips on how to navigate

So how can the social media active rising next generation avoid ruining the cherished family reputation? What is the best course of action to plan, insulate and protect a family from a quick-fire reputational crisis in the digital age?

One of the first steps is to conduct awareness conversations and training around this. I always think it's a mistake to ban anyone from social media; this is rarely the answer. For many, this is part of their everyday lives, and a ban would merely alienate them from their peer group and make their social lives awkward – especially for the younger generation. No one wants to be asked why they are the only kid not on Snapchat or Instagram.

But talking them through real-life examples of how information posted online can be used against them can change their mindset – albeit very gradually. The Internet can be a force for good, but it can also be a dangerous place. In some cases, understanding the shocking threats makes young people think twice before posting online. For the rising next generation, this is critical not only because it will help to preserve the overall family's reputation, but also if they are thinking of studying in the United States or applying for a job there, because it will make them aware of the importance of their digital footprints. This latter point often chimes with young people. They may feel unconcerned about the family, but they certainly do worry – at a certain stage in life – about themselves. I once heard an expert explain that you should manage your Google profile like you do your financial portfolio. Get rid of the social platforms that don't rank and perform, and launch new ones which can showcase your achievements and further your career. The rising next generation should be continually thinking about their digital footprints, evaluating their content and managing their social media accounts.

The second area of focus should be privacy settings. These should become second nature. I am personally seeing a big shift in this area. People are generally becoming more private and using privacy settings more. But that is not always the case. We are also seeing some generations moving more to what we call 'closed social': communicating via WhatsApp, Telegram, Signal or other chat apps on the market. That's fine; but the risk of information ending up online publicly is still the same: anyone can maliciously take a WhatsApp posting and make it publicly available, especially in chat 'groups' where people are not good friends with all users in the group.

For wealthy families, knowing what is out there online about you in granular detail is essential. A reputational crisis can arise suddenly and, like a wildfire, can spread quickly if you haven't prepared properly and don't know what to do. Knowing all about your digital footprint in intimate detail ahead of a crisis is hugely important, and allows you to respond more confidently and with greater speed. You should know your digital profile as well as you know yourself or your business.

The Deep Web, according to commonly used estimates, contains around 96% of what is out there about us and it is publicly available. The remaining 4% is indexed by search engines. Experts should conduct digital health checks on your Deep Web footprint every six months. Think of it like a check-up with the doctor. There are also great monitoring tools out there which flag content within minutes of it hitting the Internet. Families should continually monitor their footprints so that 'surface' content that appears between health checks is discovered as quickly as possible.

One example of how a family business can very quickly hit the headlines is Italy's Benetton family. It came under reputational attack from politicians and the public following the involvement of one of its companies in the Genoa bridge tragedy in 2018.[18] At least 38 people died when a section of the 1.2 kilometre-long traffic bridge collapsed, sending vehicles hurtling onto buildings and a riverbed. The bridge was part of a toll road operated by a company 88% owned by Atlantia, in which the Benetton family was the largest shareholder. Atlantia's stock devalued more than 25% in the days after the disaster. A report from Bloomberg at the time reported that $2 billion was erased from the family's net worth as the Atlantia stake was its single-largest asset, comprising more than one-third of its $13.3 billion fortune.[19]

The Benetton reputation suffered, with some social media users expressing outrage. The United Colours of Benetton ads were parodied with images of the ruined bridge and the hashtag #BoycottBenetton trended. I often wonder whether the family could ever have envisaged that such a sad tragedy might happen, how quickly it would become so destructive to the family name and how it could have prepared to mitigate this.

Finally, you can put all the measures in place to protect, monitor and mitigate against content that goes online; but there is nothing quite like something that was around long before social media – a good, old-fashioned conversation within the family.

Teaching the rising next generation about the family history, heritage and values that cement a family reputation is the bedrock. Explain the journey to a good reputation. Great families fragment, but they are often glued together by a set of values and a shared purpose. One of

"For wealthy families, knowing what is out there online about you in granular detail is essential. A reputational crisis can arise suddenly and, like a wildfire, can spread quickly if you haven't prepared properly and don't know what to do."

those values should be that togetherness cements a reputation. That may not work for Abigail Disney, who clearly has her own views on how the company that operates with her name should act; but it will for others. It is not about the 'I' in the family; it is about the 'We'. All families should think about that the next time their thumbs hover over a new social media post before pressing 'share'.

Notes

1 Yahoo News, "'I was so livid': Disney Heiress visits theme part to see worker conditions", Yahoo News (15 July 2019), https://news.yahoo.com/i-was-so-livid-disney-heiress-visits-theme-park-undercover-to-see-worker-conditions-093000722.html.

2 Jordan Valinsky, "Abigail Disney on Disney furloughs: 'What the actual f—-'", CNN Business (23 July 2020), https://edition.cnn.com/2020/04/22/business/abigail-disney-furloughs-bonus-pay-coronavirus-trnd/index.html.

3 Jim Waterson, "James Murdoch criticises father's news outlets for climate crisis denial", The Guardian (14 January 2020), www.theguardian.com/media/2020/jan/14/james-murdoch-criticises-fathers-news-outlets-for-climate-crisis-denial.

4 *Oxford Essential Quotations*, 4th edition (Oxford University Press, 2016), www.oxfordreference.com/view/10.1093/acref/9780191826719.001.0001/q-oro-ed4-00000713#:~:text=Walter%20Bagehot%201826%E2%80%9377&text=Above%20all%20things%20our%20royal.

5 "How Many People Use Social Media in 2021?", www.oberlo.co.uk/statistics/how-many-people-use-social-media.

6 Simon Kemp, "Digital 2021: Global Overview Report", Datareportal (27 January 2021), https://datareportal.com/reports/digital-2021-global-overview-report.

7 Saima Salim, "How much time do you spend on social media? Research says 142 minutes per day", *Digital Information World* (4 January 2019), www.digitalinformationworld.com/2019/01/how-much-time-do-people-spend-social-media-infographic.html.

8 Digital 2021 Global Overview Report, *We Are Social*, https://wearesocial.com/digital-2021.

9 LinkedIn, https://about.linkedin.com/#:~:text=About%20LinkedIn&text=740%20million%20members%20in%20more%20than%20200%20countries%20and%20territories%20worldwide.

10 Sky News, "YouTube deletes fly-on-the-wall royal documentary after it mysteriously resurfaces 50 years on" (29 January 2021), https://news.sky.com/story/youtube-deletes-fly-on-the-wall-royal-documentary-after-it-mysteriously-resurfaces-50-years-on-12201670.

11 Lauren Salm, "70% of employers are snooping candidates' social media profiles", CareerBuilder (15 June 2017), www.careerbuilder.com/advice/social-media-survey-2017.

12 Travel.State.Gov, "Collection of social media identifiers from US visa applications" (4 June 2019), https://travel.state.gov/content/travel/en/News/visas-news/20190604_collection-of-social-media-identifiers-from-U.-S.-visa-applicants.html.

13 Remi Cohen, "Are Gen Z-ers More Security Savvy Online than Millennials?", F5 Labs Application Threat Intelligence (13 February 2020), www.f5.com/labs/articles/threat-intelligence/are-gen-z-ers-more-security-savvy-online-than-millennials-.

14 Adi Robertson and Russell Brandom, "Congress releases blockbuster tech antitrust report", *The Verge* (6 October 2020), www.theverge.com/2020/10/6/21504814/congress-antitrust-report-house-judiciary-committee-apple-google-amazon-facebook.

15 Alex Hern, "'I don't want to upset people': Tom Cruise deepfake creator speaks out", *The Guardian* (5 March 2021), www.theguardian.com/technology/2021/mar/05/how-started-tom-cruise-deepfake-tiktok-videos.

16 Omar Oakes, "'Deepfake' voice tech used for good in David Beckham malaria campaign", *Campaign* (9 April 2019), www.campaignlive.co.uk/article/deepfake-voice-tech-used-good-david-beckham-malaria-campaign/1581378.

17 "FBI warns deepfakes could be the next major cyber threat", *The Global Herald* (13 March 2021), https://theglobalherald.com/news/fbi-warns-deepfakes-could-be-the-next-major-cyber-threat/.

18 Alexandra Newlove and James Beech, "Benetton family targeted over Genoa bridge collapse", CampdenFB/Campden Wealth (17 August 2018), www.campdenfb.com/article/benetton-family-targeted-over-genoa-bridge-collapse.

19 Devon Pendleton and Tommaso Ebhardt, "Benetton wealth Falls $2 billion after Italy bridge collapse", *Bloomberg Quint* (21 August 2018), www.bloombergquint.com/business/benetton-fortune-drops-by-2-billion-after-italy-bridge-collapse.

IV. #GenerationNow: resolving intergenerational conflicts through resilience and grit

Paul Hokemeyer
Drayson Mews International

1. Introduction

When Iraj Ispahani, the editor of this book, approached me about submitting a chapter on my work at the intersection of mental health and ultra-high-net-worth (UHNW) family dynamics, I was impressed with his innovative thinking and grateful for the opportunity to join him in advancing thought leadership in what has heretofore been the formulaic and musty area of family governance. For decades, professionals in the field have focused on the creation of documents such as family constitutions and bylaws that are intended to reflect family values to memorialise where families are in a specific moment in time and provide a roadmap to shepherd them forward. When a family remains rigid and fixed, these standardised forms can serve them well. But in my experience, life and the dynamic human beings who live it don't remain stagnant. They push against inertia and are constantly seeking to evolve to higher states of functioning. This is especially true today as we emerge from COVID-19 acutely aware of the fragility our health, the environment and the perniciousness of systemic injustices.

In this new world order, the value of these formulaic documents can depreciate quickly. This is especially true when an individual family member or an entire generation manifests iconoclastic personality traits that conflict with older generations. In this new reality, value is derived from understanding the living, breathing human being who exists beneath what have become hackneyed labels such as 'NextGen', 'Millennials', 'Gen Z' and a host of others that fail to recognise the idiosyncratic nature of human beings and the unique constellation that makes up their family dynamics.

My work as a mental health professional seeks to pierce these objectifying labels to embolden the ever-changing essence of our psyches so that they can thrive intrapersonally and interrelationally. The goal is to enable family members to flourish as individuals while creating deeper, more authentic and ultimately more productive family relationships by connecting them to older generations, whose members can use their station in life to provide empathetic and compassionate mentorship. I hope that you find the material in this chapter helpful as we move individually and collectively out from lessons learned in the pandemic to embrace lives of meaning, purpose and service to improve the wellbeing of humanity and to protect the world that we are privileged to temporarily live in.

2. Conflict dynamics

Although the defining features of generations change, a relational dynamic that unites them is the conflicts that arise when members of different generations fail to see eye to eye. These conflicts manifest directly through express disagreements; but they also manifest though a host of more insidious dynamics that fall into the category of indirect behaviours. In my years of working with UHNW individuals and families, I've seen these indirect behaviours play out in two key ways. The first consists of what are known in clinical terms as 'passive-aggressive behaviours'.[1] Through this behavioural pattern, a family member engages in a variety of 'non-actions' to protest to family demands. They fail to show up for their lives as responsible adults and remain stuck in the adolescent, rebellious stage of their development. An additional passive-aggressive pattern that I am frequently called in to dismantle is where family members acknowledge their commitments under family constitutions, trust agreements and provisions of family foundations, but fail to follow through with their obligations or engage with the family enterprises to the best of their abilities. In this regard, they evidence a lack of grit[2] – the capacity to tolerate short-term discomfort to achieve a long-term, superordinate goal.

The second class of indirect conflict that causes troubles in families comprises self-sabotaging behaviours that include substance abuse disorders, compulsive spending, gambling addictions and sexually acting out. Through these behaviours, the family member is constantly 'screwing up' their life through bad decisions and compulsive behaviours. They are unable to think things through and are victims of poor judgement and impulsive decisions. Often these

"Although the defining features of generations change, a relational dynamic that unites them are the conflicts that arise when members of different generations fail to see eye to eye."

behaviours run against family, religious and community standards. The net result is that the family gets trapped in a toxic cycle of shame, guilt and isolation. Here, the family member fails to manifest resilience[3] – a constellation of personality traits that enables people to transcend challenges placed in their way and evolve to higher states of functioning.

The purpose of this chapter is to provide a resource for family members and advisers to understand the aetiology of these destructive behaviours and to provide a set of tools that can be used to dismantle them. The ultimate goal is to locate the family in a state of optimal individual and collective performance. To accomplish this objective, the following discussion is divided into three different but interrelated parts. The first consists of an explanation of the psychological constructs underlying intergenerational conflicts. Before they can be dismantled, we need to understand why these conflicts arose in the first place and how they are fed by relational dynamics. The second consists of a case study in which the issues addressed in this chapter will be embodied in a discussion of a family that I have worked with in the past. Here it is important to note that the case, like the clinical references that I use throughout the chapter, is a composition of families with which I have worked. As such, the identifying details have been judicially altered to protect the confidentiality of the families and the integrity of my relationship with them. The chapter concludes with an application of the didactic learning with the specifics of the case to enable families to move from a place of frustration and despair to a position of healing and hope.

3. Understanding psychological schemata and their impact on relational dynamics

I don't understand why my son can't just appreciate the legacy he's about to inherit. I've worked day and night to give him a charmed life and he just resents it.
– Zurich-based father of a 27-year-old son

Over the past 15 years that I have practised as a family therapist, I have heard this statement repeated hundreds of times from frustrated parents around the world. The annoyance in their voice resonates through the love and compassion that emanates from their hearts. They want with all their personal might to help their children grow and thrive, and they have thrown abundant financial resources towards their children's success; but rather than moving their children in a positive direction, their efforts backfire and their children burrow more deeply into ruts of inaction. As a result, parents feel unappreciated and disrespected. They get hijacked by anger and resentment, which in turn causes them to redouble their efforts to force their children into behavioural changes.

"The first step to dismantling any destructive dynamic is to recognise the causes that underlie it and the forces that keep it in place."

It's like she's an apple and I'm an orange.
– Los Angeles-based mother of a 23-year-old daughter

The first step to dismantling any destructive dynamic is to recognise the causes that underlie it and the forces that keep it in place. As it relates to conflicts between generations, these causes and conditions are grounded in two important psychological constructs known as the 'self-schema' and a related concept of 'locus of control'.

4. Our self-schemata
The construct of the self-schema was clinically recognised by British clinician and researcher Dr Hazel Marcus. According to Marcus:

> *Self-schemata are cognitive generalizations about the self, derived from past experience, that organize and guide the processing of the self-related information contained in an individual's social experience... (These) self-schemata facilitate the processing of information about the self (judgments and decisions about the self), contain easily retrievable behavioral evidence, provide a basis for the confident self-prediction of behavior on schema-related dimensions, and make individuals resistant to counter-schematic information.*[4]

Our self-schemata enable us to manage, edit and make sense out of the infinite interpersonal and cultural data in which we live. Through this editing process, we navigate our world and find our place in it. When done through a positive lens, our self-schemata provide adaptive value that enables us to evolve to higher states of being. They keep us from being overwhelmed by a deluge of external stimuli and enable us to stick to a path that is consistent with our goals and aspirations. In this regard, they enhance our intentionality and diminish our reactivity. But like everything in life, they also present an opposition. On the opposite side, there is a constellation of non-adaptive attributes that keeps us 'stuck' in unhealthy patterns of being and leads us to personal and relational decay. In this state, we become passive and reactive to the world around us, rather than asserting our intentions in it.

The aetiology underlying which side of this duality we tend towards depends on the messages that we have internalised in our development path, as well as our physiological make-up. In this regard, it involves a calculus of nature and nurture. As to our physiology, those of us whose central nervous systems are more vulnerable to overstimulation, known in the clinical realm as 'highly sensitive people'[5] – those who have had a traumatic experience in their past, such as an actual or perceived interpersonal abandonment or betrayal by a primary caregiver,[6] and those who have suffered early childhood

"Schemata don't just find nourishment in data that confirms them; they also reject data that contradicts them."

illnesses or concussions – are more susceptible to developing negative rather than nurturing self-schemata.[7] According to Kendra Cherry: "Each person has very different self-schemas that are influenced heavily by past experiences, relationships, upbringing, society, and culture. Who we are and our self-perceptions are heavily influenced by how we are raised, how we interact with others, and the impressions and feedback we receive from societal influences."[8]

It is important to note that our schemata are rigid and self-fulfilling. As noted by Marcus, schemata don't just find nourishment in data that confirms them; they also reject data that contradicts them. An example is a boy who is told he isn't brave by a primary caregiver. In response to this message, he will look for experiences that confirm this characterisation of his self. The internalisation of these messages will also have a predictive influence on his future by causing him to default to a perception of self as cowardly when confronted with situations that would normally invoke bravery in his peers.

I have also found that while early childhood internalisations are important, adolescence – the period of our development when we are entering puberty and defining ourselves in relationship to others – is critical to healthy self-formation. During this phase, people who are raised in families and cultures that reject and condemn fundamental truths of their identities are highly susceptible to developing defeating self-schemata. In these contexts, people look for external evidence that confirms the world as hostile and unsafe. In response, they are highly vulnerable to developing a schema of learned hopelessness[9] – a situation where they simply give up trying to assert their power to change a situation.

As this relates to the families with which I have worked, I have frequently found friction that causes conflict between generations in the following areas of adolescent development:

- Physical changes: In adolescence, children enter into an intense phase of sexual development. This can be an especially trying time for children who feel sexual or romantic attraction to members of their gender, who have intense sexual impulses or who enter puberty early.
- Intellectual changes: Adolescence ushers in new intellectual capacities. During adolescence, children can conceptualise future possibilities rather than being hostage to their present states of being. Conflict arises when children envision a future that is inconsistent with family values and traditions.
- Social changes: In adolescence, children search for an identity independent from their family. They experiment with different roles and explore different peer groups. All goes well when they conform to expected gender and socioeconomic roles; but when they don't, conflicts are quick to erupt.

During the adolescent phase, it is important that parents set boundaries and expectations that are loose enough to allow their children to experiment with their different identities while honouring their right to have an opinion about their child's choices. Central to this task is remembering that adolescence is a phase that is passed through, not one in which families are enslaved. In so doing, parents will empower their children to develop a sense of agency over their lives and develop what is known as a healthy locus of control.

5. Locus of control

She's overly influenced by social media... Keeping up with the Kardashians is more important to her than being a part of this family.
– Mother of a 19-year-old daughter in Geneva

An important psychological concept to consider when evaluating the root causes of intergenerational conflict is the psychological construct of 'locus of control.' The concept of locus of control was developed in 1954 by Julian B Rotter to explain the extent to which people feel they have control over their lives.[10] One of the best definitions I have found of the construct is as follows: "Locus of control refers to the tendency to perceive outcomes in life as a result of one's own actions and thus being within one's own control (ie, internal locus of control), as opposed to being determined by external factors, such as chance or powerful others (ie, external locus of control)."[11]

Locus of control is one of several pillars that make up our self-schemata. Through our locus of control, we establish our personal agency and determine our place in a complex world that is full of options; and like our self-schemata, this falls on a scale from adaptive and healthy to non-adaptive and pathological.

6. Internal locus of control

On the adaptive and healthy side of the scale is what is known as an *internal locus of control*. People with a robust internal locus of control feel that they are in control of their destinies. They are highly responsible for their actions and the outcome of their actions. They view setbacks as opportunities for personal growth and improvement, rather than evidence of their unalterable deficiencies. They use the time after a failure to take inventory of what they need to change in the future to succeed and are hopeful that, with some tweaks in their behaviours, they can attain mastery over the change at hand. Yes, they would be cross if they lost their fortune; but they are highly confident that they can remake it. In this regard, they evidence robust resilience in the quantitative aspects of their life.

A healthy internal locus of control is also important in the qualitative aspects of a person's existence and self-appraisal. Through it, people can manifest resilience in the wake of interpersonal and emotional challenges that come their way. A healthy internal locus of control over the qualitative aspects of her life was eloquently expressed by the 27-year-old Dutch daughter of a shipping magnate with whom I consulted. The woman came to me to help her sort through some issues in her pre-nuptial agreement after her husband of two years left her for his French tutor. She said: "You know, Dr Paul, I'm actually grateful I got this sorted out early in our marriage. I still have loads of energy and a healthy enough self-worth to tweak my life for the better. To be honest, I made a bet, but he was the wrong horse... I'll find the right one."

Rather than assuming the position of a victim, the client utilised her locus of control to make positive and resilient generalisations about herself, take stock of her life and reclaim her place in it. As this relates to her self-schema, she was able to find substantial data to confirm her identity as a sexually viable woman with physical, emotional and financial resources that she could steward to move herself to a higher, more rewarding state of being. She rejected data that was inconsistent with this self-view and in so doing, avoided being pulled down by a narrative of victimhood: "Look, God bless him and his love interest. I'm in the market for one myself."

7. External locus of control

On the non-adaptive and unhealthy side of the locus of control spectrum are people who manifest what is known as an 'external locus of control'. In contrast to people with strong internal loci of control, people whose self-schemata are heavily weighted on the side of an external locus of control feel powerless over outside forces. They have a difficult time charting out a course and following it to completion. They don't know whether people like them for who they are or for the upholstery that surrounds their life. They have a fragile sense of self and are easily swayed by outside influences. Too often, they view their wealth and position as burdens that weigh them down, rather than as resources to be harnessed to create a meaningful life. They would be devastated if they lost their wealth and clueless as to how to regain it on their own resources.

According to Cherry, people who evidence self-schemata influenced by an external locus of control are possessed of the following features:

- They credit luck or chance for any successes they might experience;

"A healthy internal locus of control is also important in the qualitative aspects of a person's existence and self-appraisal. Through it, people can manifest resilience in the wake of interpersonal and emotional challenges that come their way."

- They believe that they are powerless to change their situation or alter the course of their future; and
- They become despondent and immobilised in the face of problematic circumstances.[12]

People with an external locus of control are constantly comparing their nascent efforts to the Herculean accomplishments of their parents and other successful ancestors. In the process, they allow their external locus of control to quash their motivation and ambition. One young man – a third-generation scion to a billion-dollar European pharmaceutical fortune whom I was treating for depression and a cocaine addiction – expressed his external schema as follows: "I'm like 'Why bother? Why do I even need to get out of bed?' I mean, nothing I'm going to do will ever live up to my family legacy." Another very clever and capable French woman I was treating for anxiety stated with dismay, after she was honoured by a women's empowerment charity: "They only picked me because of my family's ability to give them a six-figure gift. Trust me, absent that, they wouldn't even know I exist."

8. When internal and external loci of control collide

Over the years, I have found that families which experience elevated and immutable levels of intergenerational conflict also experience elevated intergenerational dissonance in their loci of control. Typically, this manifests in situations where Generation 1 (G1) has a robust internal locus of control and subsequent generations are governed by external loci of control. As I stated in an interview with Campden Wealth:[13]

> *Typically, G1 is defined by something that's called an internal locus of control. They feel much more in charge over their lives. Many G2s however, have what's called an external locus of control, so they don't quite know who they would be if they didn't have their surname or their trust fund or their bank account or they didn't go to this particular school or live in this particular neighbourhood or holiday in this particular island. Their sense of identity is tied to things that are external from themselves. If you try to impose G1 expectations on a G2 generation, you're always going to get a disconnect.*

The intersection of self-schemata and locus of control relates to generational differences in the following way. A G1, entrepreneurial wealth creator who transcends great odds to amass a fortune will internalise the message of being the master of their destiny. Their self-schema will seek out even the minutest evidence of their success to fuel their commitment to continue on with their endeavours. They will actively seek out triumphs as confirmation of their abilities and

"Families which experience elevated and immutable levels of intergenerational conflict also experience elevated intergenerational dissonance in their loci of control."

reject any data that is inconsistent with this narrative of success. Some of the best examples of this dynamic are found in the realm of politics. They include figures such as Hillary Clinton and Donald Trump in the United States, Nicholas Sarkozy in France and Benjamin Netanyahu in Israel. These individuals reject any suggestions of personal or professional failings in the face of personal humiliation and continue on, claiming entitlement to what they see as their absolute right to be public leaders.

This stands in sharp contrast to a family member from a subsequent generation who interprets the improbable odds of G1's success as evidence of *their* personal weakness. Their self-schema focuses on the impossibility of their endeavours rather than their opportunities. They constantly challenge any suggestion of opportunities that they should take or directions they should move in; and they skirt any responsibility for their actions by assuming the role of victim. Often, they blame outside forces for their situation. This includes claims of injustice, bias, prejudice or the incompetence of others. One 33-year-old client with whom I was consulting in London for his lack of direction in life would constantly argue with suggestions that I made to interject structure into his day. In response to my suggestion that he set an alarm to rise before noon, he stated: "I can't tolerate alarms. They give me migraines." When I observed that it was perhaps the late nights he spent at Cirque Le Soir that needed to be dialled back, he retorted: "You don't understand how we Europeans live because you're American. I think it's time for me to find a cleverer therapist."

It doesn't take a PhD to see how these very divergent self-schemata clash in dramatic ways. People with self-schemata of personal power and a robust internal locus of control who view their selves as masters of their destiny simply can't understand why a family member with a self-schema of diminished power and an external locus of control doesn't just pull themselves together, marshal their resources and get on with their life. Their view is, "If I did it, then you can too." Through the lens of their personal schemata, they feel a host of negative and hostile emotions towards their conflicting family, including betrayal, resentment, frustration and shame. Simultaneously, the family member with a self-schema of diminished power and an external locus of control feels unfairly criticised, emasculated and infantilised. In response, they develop resentment towards family members who challenge them and engage in a host of acting-out behaviours that push them personally deeper into paths of destruction and relationally further away from family members who love them and want them to succeed.

"Holding space for another person's truth is effective because it pierces polarising labels of 'other' that are endemic to conflicts and unites people through the vulnerability of their humanness."

Case study

Irina is a 24-year-old woman, born in Russia but raised in the United Kingdom, who entered therapy on the instance of her parents to help her 'get over' her lesbian sexual orientation. At the time of our engagement, Irina was living in Paris on a $35,000 monthly allowance that her parents provided in their 8th arrondissement flat. Initially, Irina was resistant to treatment, but agreed so that her parents would "laisse-moi tranquille" *("leave me alone") and keep her allowance flowing. In short order, I discovered that Irina felt very unloveable. This negative self-schema played out in a host of destructive ways, including drug and alcohol abuse, compulsive spending, an obsession with tattoos and relationships with abusive women.*

As a child, Irina was treated as a princess by her parents and their abundant staff. Her parents reported that everything was "going well" with Irina until she hit puberty. In London, she attended the Lycée International de Londres Winston Churchill, *where she did moderately well; but she barely made it through university at a US state college. In working with Irina, I discovered that it was during adolescence that she found herself sexually and romantically attracted to other women. Knowing that her feelings exposed her to rejection by her parents, she suppressed her feelings as best she could, but soon found herself feeling "hopeless" and profoundly depressed. In her first year at university, Irina took an enormous risk and sent a letter to her parents in which she explained her lesbian feelings and suicidal ideations. Terrified for their daughter's safety, her parents had a highly emotional response, telling her that "No one will love you as a lesbian." The family has been in conflict since over a host of issues, including Irina's "refusal to settle down and start a family" and failure to "show respect" for her parents, who feel they support her in a very generous fashion.*

What becomes immediately apparent in this case is the heart-breaking nature of the conflict, its complexity and the highly sensitive way it needs to be addressed. While some of the issues it raises may be disagreeable, I hope that you can feel the pain they visit upon *everyone* involved in the family and see that every member of the family holds a valid position that deserves to be honoured and heard.

The capacity to hold the idiographic reality of an individual's experience – especially experiences that we do not fully understand – is the touchstone of effective psychotherapy. It also provides the foundation for healing persistent family conflicts. Holding space for another person's truth is effective because it pierces polarising labels of 'other' that are endemic to conflicts and unites people through the vulnerability of their humanness. Through this technique, the person struggling in one polarity of a conflict is given an opportunity to connect with the humanness of the person alienated by the polarity of its opposition. Over the years, I have found that the mere act of becoming willing to hold space for the other person's truth without commenting, criticising or questioning it provides therapeutic value. It brings people out of isolation and into the nurturance of inclusion. As I discussed in my book *Fragile Power*: "(a)t the core of human pain is isolation from others and ourselves. We find relief from this pain in reparative human connections where we are seen and heard as vulnerable human beings."[14] This ability to piece the veneer of 'others' is important to wellbeing in our hyper-connected world of opposing political ideologies; but it is essential for the health and generativity of our families of origin. To resolve deep and persistent family conflicts, family members must have a clear understanding of the estranged family member's lived experience and the self-schema that serves as a catalyst for their perceptions and behaviours.

9. Theories in action

As this relates to the case above, my initial engagement with the family involved working individually with each member to earn their trust and assisting them to understand their individual schemata. Once these elements were in hand, I engaged the family as a group to cultivate individual empathy and deepen collective compassion. To accomplish this objective, each member of the family applied their self-schema to the collective family unit and the individuals of whom it was comprised.

To this end, I engaged each family member in the same process that I utilise when I start working with a new individual patient. This consists of an exercise in which I make a rough outline of my patient's self-schema in the following four areas of their being:

- Intrapersonal: This domain looks at the person's base level of self-esteem and motivation. It seeks to understand the narrative that they tell themselves about their self. Do they see themself as fundamentally flawed or fundamentally good?
- Interpersonal: It is important to understand how the family members view themselves in relationships with others. Are they introverts or extroverts? Do people fill them up or drain them? Are people meant to be used or treated with respect and dignity?
- Professional: Here, I seek to understand how family members view endeavours that require skill, discipline and commitment. Can they channel challenges to maximise outcomes or are they discouraged by them?
- Spiritual: In this domain, I seek to understand the person's view of religion and god. Are they atheists or do they have a spiritual belief system that guides them? Is their god loving or punishing?

Through this process, Irina's parents began to see that their daughter was not acting against them and their values, but rather being compulsively pulled towards her self-schema of feeling fundamentally flawed, unworthy of love and destined to be punished. In turn, Irina was able to see that her parents were not rejecting her, but being ruled by abject fear that the person they loved most in the world was at risk due to an identity they didn't fully understand. While this initial awareness did not immediately resolve their conflicts, it did enable the family to recalibrate their relational dynamics on a frequency of love rather than fear, compassion rather than judgement and empathy rather than rejection. Most importantly, it began their liberation from relational conflict and filled them with hope that their future could be different.

10. Conclusion

At the time of writing, the world is on the cusp of a return from disorder caused by the COVID-19 pandemic. While many issues remain obscure, one thing is clear: we are emerging from the pandemic different people from the selves who entered it.

The lockdowns and shelter in place orders that were issued during the past year have caused us to spend unprecedented amounts of time in isolation. Those of us who lived in a state of perpetual motion before

"Most of us – people who prior to the pandemic had led cluttered lives – began to see the value of an edit. We quietened the voices in our heads that craved more and savoured the richness in the extant value of what and who sat before us."

the pandemic found ourselves fixated on the immediacy of our lives and the fragility of our wellbeing. During the pandemic, relationship stresses that used to just annoy us transmuted into major conflicts. Brief periods of melancholy that we could previously brush off morphed into acute depression and paralysing anxiety. For some, the stress of the pandemic caused marriages to crumble, families to implode and businesses to teeter on the edge of annihilation. A few of my patients experienced all of these challenging events at once. But the pandemic also enabled us to manifest incredible resilience and grit. Most of us – people who prior to the pandemic had led cluttered lives – began to see the value of an edit. We quietened the voices in our heads that craved more and savoured the richness in the extant value of what and who sat before us. In short, we adapted by cultivating a schema of 'the slow and steady champion wins the race' and an internal locus of control that allowed us to maximise our intentionality and find meaning in the disruption.

Many people have been asking me, "But will these changes last?" My response to their question reflects the sobriety of a scientist and the optimism of a human being. In order for the reparative adjustments that we have made to endure, we must find a stage to stand on. We must continue to hone our voice to a pitch that suits a solo performance while enabling us to participate gracefully in a choir; and most importantly, we must continue to expand the audience that we can serve. The pandemic, while certainly stressful, has provided a once-in-a-lifetime opportunity to each and every generation that occupies this earth to repair; but it presents an exceptional opportunity for generations who are coming into their positions of power. For these women and men, the world they are about to re-enter has been humbled. It is looking for new leadership who understand the importance of environmental stewardship, that black lives matter and that women make exceptional leaders. It is crying out for individuals who seek to unite through empathy and compassion, rather than dividing by prejudice and greed. In short, it is looking for you to make a difference. Before the opportunity passes, raise your hand and step up on the stage.

Notes

1 Counselling Directory, "What's worrying you? Passive aggressive behaviour", www.counselling-directory.org.uk/passive-aggressive.html#:~:text=Commonly%20described%20as%20non%2Dverbal,often%20make%20the%20problem%20worse.

2 JM Jachimowicz, A Wihler, ER Bailey and AD Galinsky, "Why grit requires perseverance and passion to positively predict performance", Proceedings of the National Academy of Sciences of the United States of America, 2 October 2018, www.ncbi.nlm.nih.gov/pmc/articles/PMC6176608/#:~:text=Although%20grit%20is%20defined%20as,a%20key%20component%20of%20grit.

3 SM Southwick, GA Bonanno, AS Masten, C Panter-Brick and R Yehuda, "Resilience definitions, theory and challenges: interdisciplinary perspectives", *European Journal of Psychotraumatology* 2014, www.ncbi.nlm.nih.gov/pmc/articles/PMC4185134/.

4 Hazel Markus, "Self-schemata and processing information about the self", *Personality and Social Psychology*, Vol 35(2), American Psychological Association, 1977, https://web.stanford.edu/~hazelm/cgi-bin/wordpress/wp-content/uploads/2011/02/1977_Markus_Self-Schemata-and-Processing-Information-About-the-Self.pdf.
5 Psychology Today, "Highly Sensitive Person", www.psychologytoday.com/intl/basics/highly-sensitive-person.
6 Adriano Schimmenti, "Unveiling the hidden self: Developmental trauma and pathological shame", Vol 18(2) *Psychodynamic Practice*, pp195–211, 2012, www.tandfonline.com/doi/abs/10.1080/14753634.2012.664873.
7 EJ Beadle, T Ownsworth, J Fleming and D Shum, "The impact of traumatic brain injury on self-identity: A systematic review of the evidence for self-concept changes", Vol 31(2), *Journal of Head Trauma Rehabilitation*, March/April 2016, https://pubmed.ncbi.nlm.nih.gov/26098262/.
8 Kendra Cherry, "Self-schemas in psychology", Verywell Mind (9 May 2020), www.verywellmind.com/what-is-a-self-schema-2795026.
9 Jayne Leonard, "What is learned helplessness?", *Medical News Today* (31 May 2019), www.medicalnewstoday.com/articles/325355#:~:text=Learned%20helplessness%20is%20a%20state,opportunities%20for%20change%20become%20available.
10 Julian B Rotter, "Generalized expectancies for internal versus external control of reinforcement", Vol 80(1), *Psychological Monographs: General and Applied*, pp1–28, 1966, https://doi.apa.org/doiLanding?doi=10.1037%2Fh0092976.
11 I Reknes, G Visockaite, A Liefooghe, A Lovakov and S Einarsen, "Locus of control moderates the relationship between exposure to bullying behaviors and psychological strain", *Frontiers in Psychology*, 10: 1323, 6 June 2019, www.ncbi.nlm.nih.gov/pmc/articles/PMC6563764/.
12 Kendra Cherry, "Locus of control and your life", Verywell Mind (7 December 2019), www.verywellmind.com/what-is-locus-of-control-2795434.
13 James Beech, "Investing in good mental health and family relations makes business sense", CampdenFB/Campden Wealth (10 November 2019), www.campdenfb.com/article/investing-good-mental-health-and-family-relations-makes-business-sense.
14 Paul L Hokemeyer, *Fragile Power: Why Having Everything is Never Enough* (Hazelden Publishing, 2019), www.amazon.com/Fragile-Power-Everything-Lessons-Treating/dp/1616497645.

V. Women: wealth and self-reliance

Philip Marcovici
The Offices of Philip Marcovici Limited

Caroline Underwood
Philanthropy Company

1. Introduction

Women always end up with the money.
– Philip Marcovici[1]

In earlier chapters, this Special Report has focused on the importance of the grit and resilience needed to live a purposeful life. But if our focus is all about purpose and becoming the best citizens we can be in our families, our communities and our lifetimes, what role does protecting our wealth have in our long-term thinking? And what is wealth protection? Does this go beyond just managing our money?

Responsible families help all family members to contribute to the stewardship of family businesses and wealth. A focus on issues relevant to women in the family can be a critical, but often neglected, step in the asset protection and succession process. Women have a particular contribution to make to families in helping to ensure smooth succession and the protection of family businesses and wealth.

But before a family member can truly contribute to the family group, the 'We' of family, they need to be confident and self-reliant in relation to the 'I' – meaning that it is valuable to focus on ensuring that women in the family are particularly secure and self-reliant regarding family finances.

In an era when equality between the genders has moved so far forward, it seems a bit jarring to write about the specific challenges that exist for women in organising wealth; why on earth is this any different for women than for men?

In other words, why should women think differently from men about wealth and the acquisition of assets?

There are some compelling (and somewhat sad) answers to these questions:

- Women tend to live longer than men;
- In general, women have less ownership of assets than men; and
- Women are often less prepared than men about wealth protection.

But there is a view expressed by one of the authors of this chapter, Philip Marcovici, that women always end up with the money.

Let's take a look at that.

According to the World Health Organization, women generally live longer than men – on average by six to eight years. We say 'generally', but acknowledge of course that in some settings – in particular, in parts of Asia – the biological advantages of women are overridden by discrimination against women so that life expectancy of women at birth is equal to that of men. In more than 35 countries, life expectancy for women is around 80 years old; while in some parts of Africa, it is only 54 and often lower due to HIV/AIDS and maternal mortality.[2]

More baby girls survive to their first birthday than boys. But curiously – and importantly in the context of discussions about wealth – women's longevity most shows itself in old age. Research is not conclusive as to how much of this is due to lifestyle choices or relatively lower rates of cardiovascular disease and cancer. (What is clear is that smoking has a massive impact on reducing lifespan for both genders.) Women living longer means that they are often the inheritors of family wealth and businesses; they therefore often represent the older generation in the family longer than male family members. This carries both risks and opportunities for wealth-owning families.

However, despite the longevity of women, women tend to own less in the way of assets than men. Conversely, women hold a vast amount of wealth in the world. Some estimates show that one-third of the world's wealth is under the control of women.[3] And they are increasing their wealth faster than in previous decades. Apart from ownership of wealth, women play a critical role in the stewardship of wealth: around the world, women are often the decision makers charged with overseeing family finances and dealing with disputes among the younger generation.

Being prepared for these roles is critical.

In his book *The Destructive Power of Family Wealth*, Marcovici points out that "wealth can and should be a positive thing for wealth owning families and the societies they live in".[4] He goes on to discuss some of the issues that he sees as critical for families in relation to women.

Despite increasing gender equality, difficulties still regularly arise, given the lack of knowledge about money that women in families sometimes suffer. Whether in marriages or otherwise, women – like men – need to know and understand the practicalities to do with money to protect themselves and their families.

In a marriage or other relationship, a woman should be asking herself whether she knows exactly what would happen if her partner died or became severely disabled, or if the marriage otherwise came to an end. If a woman has no idea of how much money her husband has and where the money is, in a divorce or on the death of her husband, there is a mess to sort out, and the possibility of the widow or divorced wife

"In a marriage or other relationship, a woman should be asking herself whether she knows exactly what would happen if her partner died or became severely disabled, or if the marriage otherwise came to an end."

being left in difficult financial circumstances becomes a very real and oft-repeated risk. Where the wealth is with the woman, understanding how that wealth can be protected in a divorce or other marriage breakdown is critical.

For wealth-owning families, educating children to understand what they need to know about wealth and marriage and the risks that are inevitable is very important. It is not only daughters who need to know how to protect themselves and how to ensure that they are financially independent in their relationships; all family members need this knowledge, allowing them to be better spouses and better parents as a result.

As we show in this chapter, the information and support to manage your finances and protect your wealth, whoever you are, are easily accessible and well worth the trouble it takes to acquire them.

2. Why is financial and wealth planning advice different for women than for men?

When we started investigating this subject, we assumed that women and men would be pretty equal in their knowledge and management of money in a domestic, business and family wealth setting.

But we were wrong.

It turns out that the traditional view of women knowing about money, particularly in a family or domestic setting, is that men often take the lead in managing money.

Why is advice for women different from men's financial and wealth planning advice? Surely it is the same? Well, yes, it is in broad terms; but our premise is that as women, there are questions that you need to know the answers to. And in families that are still patriarchal, the importance of the women in the family to the long-term sustainability of family wealth and business is not always well respected or understood. This makes it important for the women in the family to sometimes take the lead in asking the right questions: questions that can lead to greater security for both the individual women in the family and the family as a whole – again, the 'I' and the 'We'.

> ***My mother, who is still whip smart in her mid 80s, told me that her mother – a prominent professional scientist who authored a book about optometry under a man's name – said to her, "Don't talk about money darling, it is so vulgar."***

This certainly was true – but is it really true for the current generation of young women? Shockingly, it seems so.

"In families that are still patriarchal, the importance of the women in the family to the long-term sustainability of family wealth and business is not always well respected or understood."

Daily assumptions and stereotypes aside, it is true that some women need a little bit more coaching; across many cultures, there is a tendency to 'leave it to the man'. Some even say that there is a tendency in men to think that they know how to run money better than women!

While significant progress has been made in terms of equality, in almost every culture there still seems to be a common thread that women tend not to know as much about family financial affairs as they need to.

3. The challenge of money and family

Family love is messy, clinging, and of an annoying and repetitive pattern, like bad wallpaper.
Friedrich Nietzsche[5]

There is no question of the importance of family and those people lucky enough to have a loving family have a natural advantage in life.

But it is also true that families are, in general, messy – and with the prevalence of divorce, messy in a way that previous generations did not have to unravel.

This makes it even more important to equip yourself with the right information about finances – not just for yourself, but for those around you. As a woman, you should know exactly what your financial situation will be if circumstances change; and sadly that in the main means illness, divorce or death. What will happen financially if your partner becomes seriously ill? What will happen if you become seriously ill?

The very worst time to have money discussions with the family is late at night or at a family occasion. Set aside planned time to sit with the family and discuss money.

It is up to the wealth holders – perhaps Mum and Dad – to make it clear what the situation is. But it is also up to women, as daughters, nieces, wives and sisters, to ask the right questions – and to appreciate that parents or other older generation members may not always have all the answers.

We do not suggest suddenly raising questions at a family event when tensions may already be running high, but instead setting a sensible time to ask questions calmly to get an overall picture of the family assets and finance. Sometimes this is best done between families in

"Engaging an independent and objective expert to help the family work through questions and challenges can be extremely effective – and can help to smooth any emotional outbursts or long-running tensions."

an office setting and for anyone – particularly couples – we recommend that time be put aside to do this calmly, perhaps at the dining table (and without young children present).

Having a discussion that is well facilitated can be extraordinarily helpful; here the dining table discussion might become a 'family retreat' that covers what all family members should know. Engaging an independent and objective expert to help the family work through questions and challenges can be extremely effective – and can help to smooth any emotional outbursts or long-running tensions. The best-prepared wealth-owning families are those that take steps such as these to prepare family members for their roles.

There is no doubt that conversations need to be age appropriate, from teenagers to the older generation. But the point is that women need to understand their own situation and know how to navigate a world with many possible financial pitfalls.

The undeniable truth is that by not making a plan, you are making a plan.

A study conducted by Merrill Lynch Wealth Management Research[6] revealed that 85% of women make day-to-day financial decisions. But the majority of respondents said that the male of the family "takes the lead in all major long term financial decisions like a holiday, a car, a house...".

For wealth-owning families, it is critical to think about the family's asset protection and succession strategies, and to review periodically whether what is in place still meets the family's changing circumstances. But to do this well and to properly keep an eye on advisers, all members of wealth-owning families at the right age – not only women – should be brought into an ongoing programme of learning, leading to responsibility as wealth owners. Whether a son or daughter will be involved in managing a family business or not, they need to be prepared for whatever role they will ultimately have – even if this role is limited to being an owner of the business together with other siblings who may be involved in the day-to-day management of the business. And where there is no business, just having ownership of a portfolio of assets requires preparation and knowledge.

Learning is an ongoing process, and opportunities to learn from other families and their successes and failures can also be instructive.

Everyone in the family needs to be prepared: to resist the thousands of investment scams and poor advice out there; to understand how to navigate difficult divorces and the ever-changing regulatory world; and to work well (and safely) with the advisers they will need to help guide them.

In the case of women, there is a particular need to consider whether they are as prepared as they should be.

4. Making a game plan

So where do you start? We would advise considering some of the really difficult questions – the 'what-ifs'. These are questions about life-changing circumstances – good and bad – and about what would happen in certain situations.

It is never too early to begin to think about the ownership, stewardship and succession process, and to work out what will happen to your assets if you or other family members were to become disabled or to pass away prematurely. A 'stress test' basically means asking the 'what-ifs': "What happens to my assets if I pass away? Is whatever plan I have in place appropriate to my current circumstances and what I would like to see happen? Will what I have put in place in terms of planning be destructive of my family and wealth?"

For people who are early in their lives, perhaps in their 20s – and particularly women – relying on these questions having been raised and addressed by the older generation is often a dangerous assumption. It is up to you to take responsibility and to encourage dialogue on these important issues.

If you or a family member were to pass away suddenly, what happens to the assets owned by that person? This will depend on what structures may be in place to deal with the transition of wealth, including trusts and other vehicles. If there are wills that have been validly executed, these will also come into the picture and the laws relevant to where assets are located will be key.

But who will ensure that the right things are done, and that assets are tracked down and properly looked after and transferred? Is there an inventory of assets that has been kept up to date; and do family members or others who are meant to benefit know where they should go to get information about what to do if something happens to the wealth owner? It is pretty rare for things to run smoothly, and 'stress testing' how assets are owned and whether the asset protection and succession plan works may well mean thinking through exactly what will happen in a number of circumstances, including death, and ensuring that what is intended is what will actually take place.

Part of the stress testing is also to review whether what has been put in place might create problems in terms of those who may have expected to benefit not benefiting or otherwise. If it is intended to exclude or limit the benefit of family members or others, would it be better to clarify this before the death of the wealth owner? Managing expectations between the generations is an important part of ensuring that wealth does not destroy the family.

Stress testing the structures and approaches in place is not limited to considering what happens on death, but also what would happen in the event of disability, divorce and a number of other sudden or life-changing events that affect the assets within the family. Not all challenges to wealth come from within families – the external world is full of risk that needs to be managed and addressed.

5. Knowing what assets are involved and where they are
It is worryingly common for assets to get lost and stolen as wealth owners age and in the process of succession. How family members are meant to track assets down in the event of death or severe disability is important; as is ensuring that those who will be dealing with the assets actually know their value and what intentions there are in relation to them in the event of death.

If there are valuables kept at home or in safety deposit boxes elsewhere, will the right people find them and do the right thing with

"Managing expectations between the generations is an important part of ensuring that wealth does not destroy the family."

"In a complex world, advisers are necessary; but for the safety of the family and its wealth, it is important to ensure that all family members, including women, are in a position to properly supervise advisers."

the assets? The best protection is to ensure that those who are intended to benefit know what they should be looking for. Sometimes this is not always possible or appropriate, given the ages or positions of those involved, and here using trusts or foundations may be the best approach.

But the general guidance is to think about these things – not doing so is almost sure to be problematic at an already critical or distressing time for the family.

6. Working with advisers and family offices

Where large sums of money are concerned, it is advisable to trust nobody.
– Agatha Christie[7]

Every wealth-owning family has, in effect, a 'family office' – one or more people who handle things in and around the assets of the wealth owner. Often, the wealth owner takes care of the assets while the wealth owner is around; but is enough attention being paid to who will take over this function in the event of death or disability?

Excellent tax and succession advice may have been obtained; but are the lawyers and accountants who were involved at the outset still in the picture on an ongoing basis? Very often, the legal or tax adviser is transactional, in the sense that they may have been involved in drafting a will or setting up a trust; but as the years go by, their files become out of date or lost as they retire or move on to other careers or firms. It may be difficult to pick up the trail after the passing or disability of the wealth owner. Even the most sophisticated of families, and ones that have professionally run family offices, may not have everything set up as it should be. While it sounds a bit sad to spend a day going through exactly what would happen in the event of the death or disability of a key family member, this may be the best investment of a day that you ever make. Thinking this through is something that wealth owners should be doing regularly. It is almost inevitable that not everything is arranged as it should be, given the constant changes in assets, in family circumstances and in the regulatory and tax world.

In a complex world, advisers are necessary; but for the safety of the family and its wealth, it is important to ensure that all family members, including women, are in a position to properly supervise advisers. This means knowing how to ask the right questions; monitoring the powers that advisers sometimes seek to implement in trusts, wills and otherwise; and ensuring that the right checks and balances are in place. Simply put, advisers need to be properly supervised and powers need to be in place that allow nominated members of the family to remove and replace them.

We recommend making a list of questions that you would like answered. This list might include questions about inheritance, about financial planning, about your spouse or children. There are some excellent professional advisers who will work with you to develop your thinking, but your own networks may also be helpful. The power of female networks is well known. If you have in your network professionals who will chat with you about the questions that you have, start there. Other families of wealth may also be happy to talk through the challenges with you. Or approach your female friends who are C-suite professionals in the finance and related industries; they may be happy to talk about their own experiences and even to refer you to professional advisers. There are also some really helpful sources of information and membership bodies for you to build your knowledge – for example, SmartPurse[8] and FemaleInvest[9] both provide formal and informal learning online.

7. Communication and avoiding surprises

Know what you own, and why you own it.
– Peter Lynch[10]

Much in the way of bad feeling and risk in relation to succession planning can be avoided through ongoing communication and openness within families regarding how the succession process will proceed. As children grow older, getting their input on the succession process is valuable. The more that those who are to receive assets know about what they are meant to get and where the assets are, the safer the succession process can be.

In complex situations involving second and subsequent marriages and otherwise, avoiding surprises is part of effective planning. The destruction of relationships, litigation that follows the death or disability of the wealth owner and associated problems are more likely to occur when there are surprises that emerge when the wealth owner is gone. When everyone knows what to expect and has been given every opportunity to provide input into the process, there is much less danger of bad feeling and disputes later and, more immediately, of anxiety in the last few months or years of the wealth holder.

A very effective way to address this and ensure that communication and planning are in place is to set up family retreats. Ideally, you will hold these annually; and as younger family members mature, this is an ideal time to bring them into the discussion. The agenda should cover age-appropriate issues and allow for good discussion within families about the assets of the family and how transitions are meant to take place. We all acknowledge that medical and dental check-ups are something that we should undertake regularly; and most people have their car serviced regularly and ideally comprehensively. Assets and wealth should be treated in the same way. As we age, thorough medical check-ups become even more important – and this is also true for asset protection and succession. Looking at things regularly and comprehensively, and involving those who will benefit, are exceptionally important.

8. Navigating tax laws and making choices on asset protection
An investment in knowledge pays the best interest.
– Benjamin Franklin[11]

For many families, legally planning their affairs to minimise tax exposure is an important part of planning. But how far should one go to pay the least amount of tax possible? Is it an ethical obligation of wealth owners to pay headline rates of tax to help address wealth and income inequality and not to take steps to reduce tax exposures? Where is the line between legal tax planning and illegal tax evasion? And what of tax avoidance – something that used to be considered legal and appropriate, but which is increasingly condemned by tax authorities and others?

These are issues that families need to consider and which require good advice and input from professionals who can help wealth owners

"Whatever the view of the wealth owner on how ambitious to be in their tax planning, the key is to make informed decisions and to understand the choices that one has."

to understand the risks as well as, crucially, the legalities. Wealth owners have a responsibility to society to pay their taxes and to help in addressing inequality. However, this does not mean that tax systems and governments always have it right, or that tax systems are always fair in how they work. Wealth owners have choices on where and how they invest, where they live and hold citizenship, and when and how to transfer assets to family members and others whom they wish to benefit with their wealth. Whatever the view of the wealth owner on how ambitious to be in their tax planning, the key is to make informed decisions and to understand the choices that one has.

Is it right and ethical to protect assets from a claim of creditors or from a claim from a spouse on divorce? Should a wealth owner consider all their sons and daughters in law to be gold-diggers, as some do? There really is no obvious right and wrong here. The wealth owner should simply ensure that they understand how things work and how they can go wrong, and then make informed decisions on how best to try to have things work out the way they want them to work out.

For women in the family, it is unsafe to rely on others having asked these and other questions on your behalf. Women in all generations need to understand their own wealth ownership and, importantly, how family wealth and harmony as a whole can best be protected.

9. What Mum and Dad meant

A wise person should have money in their head, but not in their heart.
– Jonathan Swift[12]

Much of the unhappiness that arises in families in and around succession has to do with arguments about what Mum and Dad meant. Misplaced expectations, informal conversations and assumptions can all contribute to a confused understanding of people's intentions.

Dissatisfied with who among the (adult) children gets what, the disgruntled child claims that "Dad actually meant to leave that asset to me" or to have had the business run by the children in a certain way. There is great benefit in ensuring that Mum and Dad make it clear what they mean long before they are not around. Family retreats and discussions in and around the succession process can go a long way towards achieving this; and accompanying these by clear expressions of wishes in wills, trusts and other succession instruments can also be helpful in avoiding future disputes. It is not safe to assume that your children and other heirs know what you mean. Putting things in writing, explaining your thinking while you are around and inviting discussion are better ways to avoid later disputes and unhappiness. And for children, encouraging your parents to take such an approach is sometimes a necessary step.

Too many wealth owners sign will and trust documents that are put in front of them by their legal and tax advisers and do not invest time in explaining to their family the thinking behind the approach implemented. Any planning undertaken with explanations can go a long way towards avoiding later disputes. Wealth owners might also consider recording themselves to outline how they would like to see things go. With the technology to do this easily available today, why not make a video recording of what the wealth owner would like to see happen with their assets, including their businesses, and how they would like to see the next generation carry things forward? This is much more personal than just having formal papers and can help a grieving family to truly understand someone's intentions.

Even more important in the process, however, is to consider a full family discussion on the asset protection and succession plan – a discussion that allows the younger generation both to be prepared for their future roles and to share their own thoughts on how the plan can be strengthened.

10. The realities of emotions and the psychology of wealth

You can only become truly accomplished at something you love.
Don't make money your goal. Instead, pursue the things you love doing,
and then do them so well that people can't take their eyes off you.
– Maya Angelou[13]

It may sound idealistic to think that communication within families early on can go far to address many potential circumstances of unhappiness and disputes. But communication is critical to avoiding problems. In today's world of wealth owners living longer and longer, it may be worthwhile considering making transfers of wealth to the younger generation earlier, to avoid children waiting to inherit until the death of a parent. Is it right that a child should inherit only at the age of 75 when their Mum or Dad dies at 100?

It may also be idealistic to suggest that children be treated equally, and that money not be used as a means of communicating or signalling favouritism within families. There are many realities that come into this, including specific family issues, such as children who are unable to deal with wealth safely. This may raise many questions: "Is it good to give my money to children early if they are too young to deal with what they get and may squander my hard-earned resources? Is it right to treat my children equally when one of them has really not turned out well and has significant problems with substance abuse or otherwise? Will my children take care of me in my old age if I take advantage of opportunities to save on taxes by making early distributions? Will I be able to pay for the right level of care for myself over many years if I release my assets to my children too soon?"

But some of the limitations on wealth owners doing the right thing are more psychological than real: "Am I afraid that my children will not visit if I don't use my money to keep them interested in me? Am I thinking about treating my children unequally in my succession plan as a way of communicating my disappointment with one of my children?" There is a role, for many families, for psychologists and other health professionals to be part of the succession process and to help navigate the complexities that wealth-owning families face. As such, part of the stress testing of the succession process should involve questions about the psychology of money and its effect on every generation.

Is it easier just to give it all away to charity? Frankly, no... This still causes many issues for families.

Nothing related to money is easy and the work that families need to do with their wealth is ongoing. And women in the family may play a catalytic role in encouraging the kind of dialogue that can be so protective of both family relationships and family wealth.

11. In the case of family businesses
These discussions become even more critical where there is a family business. The plans to transition the business within the family are often discussed with some openness. But clarity on how the next generation's involvement in the business will work day to day seems to be overlooked with alarming frequency.

There are several questions to explore here. How and when might the family business be transitioned to the next generation? Who will run the business, within the family and/or outside the family? What is the role of other family members within the business? And what will your day-to-day role be within the business?

Most importantly, it is not only those family members *in* the business who need to be prepared for their future roles. Family members involved in the ownership or stewardship of the business are critical partners to those family members involved in more active management or ownership roles. Everyone needs to understand their rights and responsibilities if things are to work out well.

12. Divorce and security
A woman's best protection is a little money of her own.
– Clare Boothe Luce[14]

And then there is divorce. No one wants to think about divorce when their relationship is progressing happily. No one wants divorce. But it is a sad fact of life today that the expectations of previous generations of 'one job, one house, one spouse' have long been consigned to the past. Divorce is expensive and the single biggest destroyer of wealth... or is it? Often, the legal rights of spouses on a divorce are such that the divorce can *create* wealth – but does this come at the expense of a family business?

Where finances are well organised and fairly distributed, women can find themselves managing more independent wealth than they had before. Previous generations may not have had the liberty to do this – for example, one of the authors finds it extraordinary that her mother did not know how to write a cheque until her 60s, as her husband had always done this for her!

How do I know if my new partner is a gold digger? A safe answer is to hope for the best and plan for the worst. By understanding how the relevant rules work and the rights that spouses have, we can protect ourselves and the wealth and businesses we may have an interest in. For women holding the money or marrying into the money, understanding how pre-nuptial and post-nuptial agreements work and how to protect themselves and their families is critical.

Inherited assets are vulnerable in divorce, whether or not trusts are in place. It is thus very important to plan things carefully.

Women – and particularly younger women – who may be starting long-term relationships need an understanding of how these rules work and how the steps that they take in relation to their financial affairs can make a difference.

There are planning approaches that can be undertaken to protect assets in the case of divorce, and particularly opportunities for the older generation to do things that will make it difficult for the spouses of their children to make claims against assets deriving from the older generation. But not all of these work; and it is interesting to see how many cases there are of families that have lost control of substantial businesses and wealth through a lack of attention to the risks involved.

Pre-nuptial and post-nuptial agreements play an increasingly important role in the protection of wealth in the case of the break-up of a marriage or other relationship. Although they are not always a perfect fix, the laws of an increasing number of countries do recognise agreements entered into before a marriage (pre-nuptial) or after a marriage (post-nuptial) relating to the economics associated with the dissolution of the marriage.

"Family members involved in the ownership or stewardship of the business are critical partners to those family members involved in more active management or ownership roles."

It is critical to discuss pre-nuptial agreements and their usefulness very early on in the process of discussing family finances and succession within a family. If Mum and Dad put off discussing pre-nuptial agreements until their son or daughter arrives home holding hands with *the one* and, on meeting them, Mum and Dad then tell their son or daughter about pre-nuptial agreements and the necessity for them – "Er, son, can we speak in the kitchen?" – it won't be surprising if the young lover perceives the discussion as a negative judgement of the person they have brought home for their parents to meet. Much more effective is to have the discussion about pre-nuptial agreements well before the man or woman of their dreams is introduced, and to make pre-nuptial arrangements a family requirement that is communicated to potential spouses as part of the overall family governance approach, not something subjective and specifically related to them and their exciting new partner.

A woman needs the financial security to walk away whenever she wants. Make sure that you and your female dependants have enough assets to make free financial decisions at any time in your lives. This gives a feeling of security and happiness.

As a practical matter, what does this suggestion actually mean? Say that my daughter is about to marry into a fabulously wealthy family. I

"A woman needs the financial security to walk away whenever she wants. Make sure that you and your female dependants have enough assets to make free financial decisions at any time in your lives."

may have some assets that I may leave to my daughter on my death, but the amount pales in comparison to the wealth of my daughter's in-laws. In planning for succession to my assets, maybe it makes sense to consider ensuring that assets I leave to my daughter will be available to her in emergency-type circumstances only – through trusts or other planning vehicles, I might restrict her access to what I leave her, so as to ensure that the moneys are available to her throughout her life as a way to ensure that she never becomes financially dependent on her husband. If her marriage continues for 30 years and she gives up her career and only late in life comes to a divorce, my having provided financial security may make the difference in allowing my daughter to exit from a bad situation.

But you should ask yourself the 'what-ifs' about divorce too. This is difficult and painful, but could make a real difference if you find yourself in this unfortunate situation. Talking about money and the financial aspects of a marriage with your partner in advance of the marriage is a healthy thing.

What if:

- *We get divorced?*
- *Because of the divorce I will have to focus on looking after the children and it will be difficult to travel.*
- *Because of the divorce we may have to move.*

13. Finance, mental health and the new norm of living to 100 and beyond

There are many psychological issues that relate to wealth and no amount of wealth overcomes this reality. As with other areas of mental health, open discussion and getting the right assistance to navigate these issues are key. Eminent psychiatrist and author Dr Paul Hokemeyer reflects on some of these issues in his chapter in this Special Report.

Related to issues of mental health are changing demographics and the effects of these on wealth-owning families. Women have a particular role to play in families in this area, for better or for worse. Often, because women live longer, the widow ends up holding the family wealth or family business for the very long term. When assets pass to the younger generation, it may be Mum who ends up being the only survivor in the older generation, playing the role of mentor and arbitrator in disputes among the young generation. But has Mum been well prepared for these roles? And has the family been prepared for Mum taking on these roles?

Women often play the role of caregiver within families, particularly in relation to ageing parents. It is not only death that makes taking care of one's assets impossible; a variety of disabilities – including dementia and other illnesses associated with age – can affect the ability of a wealth owner to look after their affairs. Part of good succession planning is to consider who will be able to make decisions if the wealth owner is unable to make them. Stress testing the succession plan also means considering what happens if the wealth owner becomes disabled and unable to communicate; or if dementia or another disorder makes it impossible for them to make decisions about their healthcare or financial situation. In the absence of clarity on these issues, decisions may fall to those in or out of the family who, under the relevant law, can apply for the ability to make decisions in the place of the wealth owner – but is that always the right person to do this? Has the wealth owner considered that the spouse they were about to divorce may be the one who ends up with the power to make decisions over not only their assets, but whether they remain on life support?

Planning in view of the possibility of living much longer than was the case in the past is also important as a means of addressing some of the real issues that ageing wealth owners face. It is sadly common to see the elderly suffering from forms of dementia, first not remembering where they left things and soon developing a form of paranoia, suspecting staff and family of stealing their possessions. Money becomes something to hang on to, with a sense developing that it is the tie that keeps the younger generation coming to visit.

Families should discuss these dynamics openly at an early stage of their planning and clarify the approach that works best for succession in the context of their family.

14. A changing world, the needs of business and wealth owners and understanding the tools used to address those needs

Being financially literate is a powerful thing, especially for women.
– Otegha Uwagba[15]

There are many issues that women need to be aware of in relation to wealth. The first step in ensuring that you have the knowledge you need (and ensuring that your daughters also have the knowledge they need) is to understand that in a complex world, no one person – whether a professional adviser or otherwise – will have all the answers. An effective adviser will, however, be able to raise the right questions and help the family to find the answers in the right places. Stefan Liniger, an expert on advising wealth owners internationally, addresses some of these important issues in more depth in Chapter VI.

"For women in the family, having the objective of being able to ask the right questions is an important step on the journey towards self-reliance."

For women in the family, having the objective of being able to ask the right questions is an important step on the journey towards self-reliance. An effective education programme on the subject of women and wealth might cover, among other things, topics such as the following:

- The changing world that we live in affects wealth planning in many ways, and not only in relation to investment returns. Tax transparency and information exchange, political risk, new taxes associated with the post-pandemic world and much more will remain with us for years to come. Self-reliance in relation to wealth requires an understanding of the dynamics affecting not only investments, but also how wealth can be protected and preserved across generations.
- How tax systems work is important to understand, particularly in a world of mobility and where the choices made by the younger generation as to where they might study, live and work can affect family wealth and businesses and more. Tax systems also affect investment choices, as it is the after-tax, not the pre-tax, return that counts. And given that so many investments are cross-border, this requires an understanding of how tax rules apply in the home country, the country of investment and the country in which investment vehicles may be located. We do not

all need to become tax experts; but we need to be in a position to ask the right questions and to act on the answers.
- Understanding the holistic needs of the family is important. Wealth-owning families have many needs – some individual to their families, some common to all families – but it is only once needs are identified that they can be attended to. Families must navigate succession laws, which differ from country to country, and which are sometimes affected by religion. Wills, second families, asset protection, multi-jurisdictional families, conflict resolution, family business governance, philanthropy and much more come into the mix.
- The tools of wealth planning include trusts, foundations, companies, partnerships, insurance strategies, safe boxes and much more. All family members need to understand the tools employed in their family asset protection and succession structure and the roles they are meant to play. And for the younger generation – women in particular – asking questions about the checks and balances is key. Will advisers or others 'kidnap' family wealth once the matriarch and patriarch are gone? Or can younger-generation beneficiaries properly keep an eye on them and remove and replace them if necessary? Unless you raise these issues while your parents are around, the chance to influence things may be lost forever.
- In a complex world, advisers are needed; but are family members equipped not only to ask them the right questions, but also to keep an eye on fees and monitor the work they are doing? Asset managers are good at hiding the revenue they receive and masking some of their conflicts of interest – are family members equipped to manage this?

15. A five-step plan to financial self-reliance

- Know where your wealth is:
  - Make a list of your assets, include your own and shared assets.
  - Talk to your parents or other wealth holders about their financial plans.
  - Understand the plans for the family business and your role in it.
  - Review the 'what-ifs': "What if Mum or Dad passes away? What if my husband and I divorce? What if my daughter marries the wrong man?"
  - If your family asset protection and succession plan includes the use of planning tools such as trusts and foundations, understand how they work, the governance in place and your role going forward.
- Make a game plan:
  - Treat managing your money as you would managing your career.

    - Apply this to inherited and earned money.
    - Consider how you want to spend it over years – not just over months.
    - Include your inheritance plans and your philanthropic plans.
- Fall in love carefully:
    - If you are single and beginning a serious relationship, make a finance plan for yourself – before you fall in love!
    - Uncomfortable as it might seem, have a finance discussion before you are married and if necessary, put a pre-nuptial agreement in place. It may not be very romantic, but it could be game changing.
- Build a group of people you trust:
    - Trusted advisers might come in different roles, but include professional advisers in your game plan.
- Live your life with purpose and joy:
    - Having wealth is a blessing – get organised, protect yourself but above all enjoy it!

Notes

1 Philip Marcovici, *The Destructive Power of Family Wealth: A Guide to Succession Planning, Asset Protection, Taxation and Wealth Management* (John Wiley & Sons Ltd, 2016).
2 World Health Organization, "Global Health Observatory; women and health", www.who.int/gho/women_and_health/mortality/life_expectancy_text/en/.
3 Anna Zakrezewski, Kedra Newsom Reeves, "Managing the Next Decade of Women's Wealth" (BCG 2020), www.bcg.com/publications/2020/managing-next-decade-women-wealth.
4 Philip Marcovici (n 1).
5 Friedrich Nietzsche (1844–1900) was a German philosopher who became one of the most influential modern thinkers. Quote sourced from www.quotes.net/quote/16062.
6 Merrill Lynch, "Seeing the Unseen: The role gender plays in wealth management", www.ml.com/content/dam/ML/Registration/seeing-the-unseen-whitepaper.pdf.
7 Dame Agatha Christie (1890–1976) was an English writer of 66 detective novels and short stories. Quote sourced from Agatha Christie, *Endless Night* (Collins Crime Club, 1967).
8 SmartPurse is a money and coaching toolbox online focused on building the knowledge of women in relation to financial confidence and independence; www.smartpurse.me.
9 FemaleInvest is a financial educator run by women, for women; femaleinvest.com.
10 Peter Lynch (1944–) is an American investor, mutual fund manager and philanthropist. Quote sourced from Novel Investor, "Peter Lynch: The Single Most Important Thing" (11 March 2020).
11 Benjamin Franklin (1706–1790) was one of the Founding Fathers of the United States and a writer, philosopher, politician, statesman. Quote sourced from "The Way to Wealth" (1758), https://en.wikipedia.org/wiki/The_Way_to_Wealth.
12 Jonathan Swift (1667–1745) was an Anglo-Irish satirist, essayist, poet and Anglican cleric. Quote sourced from Jonathan Swift, Thomas Sheridan, John Nichols, *The Works* (1808).
13 Maya Angelou (1928–2014) was an American poet and civil rights activist. Quote sourced from www.goodreads.com/quotes/4749-you-can-only-become-truly-accomplished-at-something-you-love.
14 Clare Boothe Luce (1903–1987) was an American author, politician, and public conservative figure. Quote sourced from Clare Boothe Luce, "The Women" (1936).
15 Otegha Uwagba (1990–) is an author, journalist and speaker, included in the 2018 *Forbes* 30 under 30 list. Quote sourced from Otegha Uwagba, *Little Black Book: A Toolkit for Working Women* (Fourth Estate, 2017).

VI. The anatomy of wealth planning: a comprehensive primer for all generations

Stefan Liniger
Kaiser Partner Wealth Advisors

1. The emotions of wealth

Few things in life stir emotions quite like wealth, as you will probably know from your own experience. Whether you are a wealth owner or advise wealth owners, you will have seen how emotional the subject of wealth can become. You will have formed your own ideas on growing, owning and spending wealth. You will have seen how much power it gives individuals, for good or ill. And doubtless you will have seen how wealth can destroy people, relationships – even entire families. All of this means that talking about wealth isn't easy, whether for the older generations or for the younger ones.

1.1 In our nature

What gives wealth such mysterious powers to affect us like this? The answer lies in the anatomy of our brain and in the story of our past. Just the thought of money touches something deep and sensitive within us and can trigger unconscious, obscure memories within the subcortical regions of our mammalian brains. Why? Because it is so inextricably bound up with our survival and physical wellbeing.

In other words: the desire to possess is a primordial force and thinking about money possibly reaches the area of our brain associated with aggressive survival patterns.[1] As neuroscience tells us, the characteristic of these subcortical patterns is that they are affective[2] and therefore insatiable. On the one hand, these patterns want us to feel safe. On the other hand, they push us to want more and to fear that we can 'never have enough'. This leads to a perpetual battle in our psyche, meaning that we never truly 'feel safe'.

Think of the concept of 'hedonic hunger'. We have an emotional desire to eat sugar or fat in processed food, without any physical need. Why? Because eating sugary or fatty food triggers addictive reward circuits in our brains, which in turn prevents the hormones we need to tell our brains that we are not actually hungry from working.[3]

So in the ancient and often dominant parts of our brains, we are hunter-gatherers by nature: forever on a quest for more, never feeling entirely content. As such, it is no surprise that recent studies have shown that a high proportion of wealth owners don't feel they are wealthy, or wealthy enough, to consider themselves 'economically safe'.[4] Even in a position of economic abundance, our primal fears of starvation and death still hold remarkable sway over our emotions.

1.2 A conscious life

Of course, we can be greater than our primordial fears and desires. Our higher brain functions enable us to experience life at higher levels. We are able to reflect on our options in subtle ways through learning from the riches of our higher neocortical expansions. At that level, we are able to integrate the complexity of all the conscious and unconscious levels interacting within us,[5] moving beyond our hunter-gatherer past to think deeply about our nature and about our actual needs.[6] This enables us to live and behave more cerebrally, culturally and creatively.

The psychology of wealth is often underappreciated in the planning of wealth.

To do so when it comes to our understanding and handling of wealth, we need to understand the emotional complexities of wealth. So this is what I wish to put forward as my first point: the psychology of wealth is often underappreciated in the planning of wealth, whether it is carried out by wealth owners or wealth advisers. I find this odd because if you can think more consciously about your wealth and how it affects yourself and those close to you, you can design a system of governance that addresses these emotions head-on. You can create a wealth plan to express your true intentions, enabling you and those close to you to thrive. Because our emotions are a reality. They cannot be removed and our affective lives are not completely intertwined, let alone under the full command, of our cognitive abilities.

1.3 Embracing the emotions

Thus, wealth planning should involve as many questions to do with your emotions as your finances. How can you use wealth to create the safety we crave – for yourselves and for your loved ones? How can you provide not only a secure environment, but one where people can flourish, learn and evolve? How can you create a system that embraces you and your family's concerns or fears, and helps move beyond them? Fear not only affects the individual; it affects the entire system. If people act on fear, they are limited to the use of the affective parts of their brains, do not live their full potential and are prone to unnecessary fighting.

It goes without saying that I do not want to suggest that wealth planning becomes an unnecessary and potentially difficult deep-dive into the abysses of the human psyche. Instead, I prefer to take inspiration from American psychiatrist Irvin Yalom, who states that we find the four ultimate concerns of life – death, freedom, existential isolation and meaninglessness – in every level of human activity.[7] Hence, considering these concerns makes wealth planning a more useful process.

To share a simple example: most parents agree on a standard of food, shelter, healthcare and education for their children. But then comes the question of peer pressure and how far a child is allowed (or encouraged) to follow the behaviour of their contemporaries – usually in terms of behaviour and lifestyle. Is a Tory Burch bag for an 11-year-old essential? Or flying first class for a teenager? Some parents would say no, and that they are already generous to their children. However, the children may not agree if they cannot buy the same brands as their peers or live the same lifestyles. So we end up in a conflict, which is a financial one on its surface, but also a highly emotive one. Why?

Because deep-rooted, as human beings, we associate with other people in an effort to belong. Initially, of course, we want to belong to our parents; but as soon as we leave the age of a toddler, we are programmed by nature to follow the lead of our peers. If as parents we understand this, we will be better equipped to deal with conflict and react with more empathy. Otherwise, although the subject of dispute may seem absurd – to fly first class or economy – conversations like this can trigger unconscious, atavistic aspects of who

"MY PARENTS TELL ME I AM WORTH IT"

we are, of how much we are 'worth' to the other person; and as a result, potentially tear apart the fabric of a family. Life is complex.

1.4 The relationships beneath

To paraphrase the poet John Donne, no individual is an island. None of us exists in isolation. Every wealth owner – whether a child comparing themselves to their peers or an entrepreneur planning their succession – has relationships they care about, with family, friends, employees, political organisations, charities and so on. Each of these relationships brings an abundance of potential and actual interactions, expectations, conflicts, joys, sorrows and rewards. Together, all these experiences shape the way a wealth owner thinks about and interacts with those around them.

Beneath any wealth or succession plan are relationships.

Thus, we come to the second point of my introduction: that wealth owners (and advisers) need to appreciate the complex dynamics of these relationships, because beneath any wealth or succession plan are relationships. If you consider these within your plan, you can educate, influence and support those around you. You can foster virtues of independence, entrepreneurship and social responsibility, and help to avoid mere consumerism and self-interest.

After all, your plan reflects – consciously or unconsciously – the way you think about yourself and others. It reflects your attitudes towards other individuals, including their talents, characteristics, challenges and desires; as well as your attitudes to society as a whole. A meaningful starting point for any wealth plan is therefore to ask: how can you use wealth to improve your relationships and contribute positively to the development and lives of those you care about?

To do this, you need to understand your values – implicit and explicit, conscious and unconscious – and evaluate how your current plan facilitates (or frustrates) them. For example: how far is behavioural compliance in your current plan attached to generosity and access to wealth? How much is money used to control people within the system? To what extent does money rule (and do we want this)?

You also need to understand whether your governance structure may be in part a smoke-screen for unresolved conflicts within your family. Every family has its history and unfinished business; but the more you are aware about them, the less they control and the more there is room for empathic behaviour and for reconciling relationships. Hence, a proper wealth plan involves being brave, looking behind the curtain and taking a conscious approach to how your wealth and family will interact.

"A meaningful starting point for any wealth plan is to ask: how can you use wealth to improve your relationships?"

2. The goals of wealth planning

On the surface, wealth and succession planning may seem a purely technical subject. Countless books have been written about the instruments that enable the transition of wealth from one generation to the next. Also, there has been much recent discussion on the governance of family wealth. But before the technical aspects come a few essential strategic questions. Understand these and you will have the compass and toolkit to navigate your way through an existing or envisaged wealth plan, and to prepare for a conversation with your successors, parents or advisers. After all, the main question in any planning is: do the current or planned legal instruments actually serve their intended purpose? And, just as critically: is the system sound?

To answer these questions, you must ask a series of others:

- What do you want to achieve with your wealth – for yourself (and your loved ones), during your lifetime and beyond?
- How much do you want to give during your lifetime and how much afterwards? (Do you want to give with warm hands or cold ones, and how long is your planning horizon?)
- How do you want to give? With outright ownership to your successors or through legal instruments (eg, trusts which serve as a custodian for future generations, giving access and potentially income)?

- Whom do you want to give to and on what conditions? How can you make sure that your wealth will empower, not spoil? Likewise, how can you avoid being too miserly?
- Who is in charge, now and after your lifetime? What are the checks and balances to ensure a proper division of powers, rights and responsibilities?

Do the current or planned legal instruments serve their intended purpose?

2.1 Beyond the technicalities

Of course, we all know that asking such questions (and finding practical answers) is essential to the success of any wealth plan. But for most of us, thinking about legal tools and governance mechanisms is – understandably – rather technical (and boring). What's more, thinking about wealth planning also entails thinking about tricky subjects such as the following:

- anticipating the needs of current and future generations;
- organising an orderly succession;
- considering global mobility and the implications of living internationally;
- meeting the ever-expanding standards of global compliance;
- protecting assets;
- reputation and privacy management in an increasingly transparent world;
- family, business and investment governance;
- contingency and continuity planning;
- preserving and growing wealth; and
- charitable giving.

It's a lot to consider. And so it's no surprise that sometimes we can struggle to see the wood for the trees – particularly as for some entrepreneurs, business and private life are one, making separating these subjects a difficult process.

But wealth planning doesn't have to be boring or overly technical. Instead, it can feel practical and grounded in everyday reality. Imagine, instead of answering technical questions around governance or planning, you were asked questions such as the following:

- What would happen if a family member died or became incapacitated tomorrow?
- What if the key people in a business were to die today?
- How are all family members protected?
- Are the heirs ready for the assets (and are the assets ready for the heirs)?

- Would the current succession plan lead to conflicts within the family or business?

Suddenly, now that it has moved from the abstract into the human, you may find that your appetite for wealth planning increases.

2.2 Uncomfortable emotions

Succession planning can be emotionally draining and uncomfortable too. After all, who wants to face their own mortality? Who wants to talk about the risk of divorce when a new partner joins the family? Who wants to bring up the spectre of potentially dysfunctional relationships between family members?

True, these are sensitive moments. And true, they may lead to some difficult conversations. But the alternative can, in my opinion, be far worse. If you plan without considering the impact on those around you, on your family or business, you risk damaging the very fabric that keeps your loved ones together. And if you plan without a proper enquiry into what your loved ones need to thrive, you risk spoiling them or hampering their instinct for self-affirmation and self-respect. It is essential to consider the psychodynamic perspective in any wealth plan, so that your actions unite and reconcile, rather than risk further division.

Consider the psychodynamic perspective in any wealth plan – to unite and reconcile, rather than to risk further division.

2.3 An inclusive, cross-generational dialogue

Take planning for the younger generation. This is not, as some imagine, simply the preserve of the older generations, or a 'one-way street' where the older generation help prepare the younger.[8] In fact, older members of the family may need just as much preparation to help build and implement a wealth plan.

Needless to say, I don't propose that this should be a democratic process, with each family member holding equal sway. And true, there is the well-known problem of 'spoilt' younger generations, of feelings of entitlement to a certain lifestyle and the phenomenon of 'affluenza'.[9] This is exactly why it is so important to involve younger generations in the planning process. In the workshops and retreats I lead, I encourage older members – sometimes through role play – to take the perspective of younger members and vice versa. Through this, they can come to experience and realise the different generations' views, hopes, expectations and fears in a non-confrontational (and often fun) manner. This can create emotionally engaging moments, increase alignment and strengthen empathic relationships – especially when the common understandings (or disagreements) are translated into specific definitions of clear values, and into the allocation of roles and responsibilities.[10] After all, a plan isn't just to protect wealth for the next generation: it's also to protect the next generation from wealth, and the potentially destructive impact of being born into a wealthy family. For your plan to succeed over the long run, you need to ensure that each family member individually and the family as a whole transition and use wealth wisely.

Planning also involves protecting the next generation from adverse impacts of wealth.

2.4 Into the long grass

Hence, there will always be reasons to delay wealth and succession planning; to kick, as they say, the subject into the long grass; and to believe there will be plenty of time later on to tackle these issues. But life, as we all know, does not happen on the drawing board. Instead, planning tends to be at the mercy of events: buying a new home; creating or selling businesses; moving abroad; having children; falling ill; and eventually, dying.

As such, we tend to think that all of these individual plans will naturally form one cohesive whole. But this is seldom the case, since the individuals (or advisers) charged with those individual plans rarely have the full picture. Plus, legal and fiscal legislation is always in flux, requiring not only careful monitoring, but also a well-balanced team of specialists to ensure that the plan is not driven purely by one aspect, such as business succession or tax, at the expense of others, such as family or investment governance. That is why it is so important to gain an overall perspective, join the dots and consider your 'Plan B' (what happens if a heart attack or plane crash barges into your life?), instead of delegating to lawyers, tax advisers or financial advisers, with inevitably incomplete knowledge of your situation, to create a comprehensive plan that engages all areas of your life.

2.5 Giving purpose by creating your legacy[11]

We are all searching for meaning. As Holocaust survivor Viktor Frankl said, life is never made unbearable by circumstances, but only by lack of meaning and purpose, which cannot be given arbitrarily, but must be found responsibly.[12] This desire to find and give meaning only strengthens as we grow older and we think increasingly about what we will leave behind. In this context, it can be helpful to ask yourself the following questions:

- What legacy do I want to create?
- How can I enhance and preserve my family values for future generations?
- How can I care for those close to me (and for those who may be in need)?

- What rules will govern access to family wealth?
- How can I educate and encourage loved ones to earn, save and be charitable?
- How can I shift family members from self-interest to mindfulness?
- What holds a family together over the long run – in times of economic crisis in the family or intergenerational conflict?

Asking these questions helps to define the basic values of how a family interacts, operates and resolves conflicts. It gives purpose and provides a foundation for future generations, and a compass to guide individuals and the family.

3. Understanding your assets
Naturally, to create a proper plan for your wealth, you must understand how much wealth you have. This may not always be as straightforward as it seems and involves three main considerations.

3.1 How much do you want to tell your family?
Transparency is key to any understanding of family wealth. But for some, this is a tricky issue. In an unstable world, some parents may be cautious about sharing details of their exact wealth with their children. Ultimately, it comes down to two sets of questions. What if the younger generation become unmotivated in life once they know how much wealth the family has? Will their partners and spouses become a threat? Contrarily, if there is no transparency, how can the family be protected from advisers or others who are close to the wealth owner – and who may take advantage of their position? There are countless stories about advisers, trustees and business partners who, after a wealth owner died, abused their powers, walked away with assets which were intended for the family or kept them hostage.

Likewise, how can you protect your children from unrealistic expectations if they don't know the size of your wealth? After all, they may get used to a certain lifestyle while you are alive that they simply will be unable to afford if your estate is divided multiple times.

3.2 How should you approach informal arrangements?

This is particularly relevant for first-generation wealth or in countries with high political risk. A wealth owner may hold assets through nominee arrangements, which entail a high risk of loss of control. Or they may be in business with no formal shareholder agreement between business partners, including contingency plans and rules on business succession.

Scenarios such as these can pose a serious risk for spouses, partners, children and other successors to a business. That is why it's important to have a full inventory of family assets and ensure that title documents are held in a safe place. In some cases, it might also be advisable to formalise business relationships, defining terms of business succession and how family members might be introduced into the business.

3.3 How will you gain a dynamic understanding of the numbers?

Just like planning for a business, the numbers are essential for wealth and succession planning. You need a clear picture of all consolidated assets, liabilities and income – not only to understand the status quo, but also to oversee how your assets interconnect. An inventory such as this should include a budget, expense and cash-flow statement, adapted and tested for various scenarios.

Understand how your individual assets are interconnected.

It is also important to understand the role that an asset plays for the family. Is the asset:

- a lifestyle asset that is currently being used (eg, a family home)?
- an income-generating asset that needs managing (eg, a family business or investment portfolio)?
- a tangible long-term investment that, while appreciating in value, requires maintenance costs (eg, a piece of art or classic car)?

These assets need to be understood not only in light of the current family situation, but for future generations as well:

- What type of lifestyle will future generations be able to afford, based on the current family assets? (At what stage and under what conditions?)
- What if there is an economic downturn in the business or if private assets are used to secure business ventures?
- What risks need to be considered in the interdependence of individual asset classes?

How you allocate and preserve wealth will be essential to any succession plan (which normally includes an investment policy statement), along with the generation of income. That is why it's so important to wear both the strategic and practical hats of a financial planner, and look at both the underlying numbers and the overall goal of your plan.

4. How will you gain an understanding of the legal complexities?
Now come some technical aspects of planning: the legal, fiscal and regulatory considerations. These are essential to help translate your ideas and concepts into action. In a fast-changing world full of economic, political and social risks, nothing can be taken for granted. A legal framework is required to accommodate these challenges and to protect your family and wealth. To do this, you need a network of experts across a range of areas to design, implement and watch over your legal arrangements. Inevitably, this is another complex topic. But underneath the complexities are a few simple principles that help you make the process comprehensive, and I would suggest that you test your plan (and your advisers!) against these.

4.1 Avoid the artificial
First and foremost: where do you want to live and spend your time? This is the keystone of your plan, because we live in an ever more transparent, interconnected world. Think about public registers for shareholders, landowners and beneficial owners; or exchange of information and a strong political agenda to shut down inappropriate planning arrangements.

There is no room for complacency. If you (or your family) move across jurisdictions, you will need to ensure that you don't spend too much time here and there. Even if you don't like the legislation of your current residence, it's important to comply with it, right down to the last letter. Beware of advisers who might encourage you to sail close to the edges: ultimately it will be you and your family who have to face the bill.

4.2 Enable mobility; embrace diversification and complexity
Complex planning can help your family to live in peace and safety, and maintain their international mobility and security. After all, history has shown that jurisdictional and other diversification helps to protect not only the wellbeing of families, but also their business and other assets.

Diversification and risk management aren't just useful for multi-generational families: they can help first generation wealth too, where diversification tends to be lower – in terms of both assets and the location of family members.

4.3 Stress-test and anticipate risks and potential conflicts

Inside or out, there will always be potential threats to your family. From family disputes to political risks, you must constantly anticipate such risks and build in protection mechanisms.

To preserve wealth, this might include using bi- or multilateral investment protection treaties (with appropriate dispute resolution clauses). For family disputes, this could involve dispute resolution mechanisms such as mediation or arbitration. In such proceedings, privacy is normally better maintained (and reputation managed).

Your legal structures serve your purpose, not someone else's.

4.4 Engage people who join the dots

The legal side of planning can be a puzzle – and a puzzle whose pieces need to be continuously adapted and moved. This is why off-the-shelf options are no longer an option. Your legal structures should serve your purpose, not someone else's. And they should work, being constantly updated to take into account tax and legal implications.

Ensure that these legal structures are balanced and cover the technical and non-technical aspects of your planning. For this, you

"The legal side of planning can be a puzzle – and a puzzle whose pieces need to be continuously adapted and moved. This is why off-the-shelf options are no longer an option."

need a coordinated team, with a diverse range of expertise drawn from different areas, disciplines and locations. And to coordinate the team, you need a conductor: someone with a holistic perspective who can orchestrate the different elements, strategically and practically.

4.5 Stay in the driver's seat

Your legal structures should reflect your needs, values and principles. Advisers can be invaluable in asking the right questions and guiding you through the technicalities. But remember: this is *your* plan. Don't be too impressed, let alone intimidated, by advisers either. You must own the direction and content of it, and ensure that you have the right instruments in place.

5. The delicate questions around giving

Wealth planning is about protecting the people dear to you, as well as your assets. But it is also about protecting how the assets are used. And that, as with so much in life, is easier said than done. When it comes to wealth, none of us are blank slates. We have all learned to spend and save (in varying degrees) from our parents and those around us. We copy our parents' behaviour from our earliest days, so the sooner financial education starts, the better prepared we can be.[13] Any later behavioural changes are complex and can be easily thwarted. For example, you may have reached an agreement with your child on how much they can spend, only to find it disrupted by overly generous grandparents. Or you may find that you disrupt it by your own hand, by being inconsistent with your rules or resolutions.

Wealth planning is also about protecting how assets are used.

In this context, wealth owners and parents face a series of questions:

- How much money do you give to each family member? When and in what way?
- What conditions do you set? Do you reward academic achievements or the 'good boys and girls' whose behaviour you approve of?
- Do you give the same amounts to everyone, regardless of their role in the family, but with the preservation and growth of the family assets in mind?[14]

Each family will have their own answers. But in any event, it is important to build learning opportunities into each stage. After all, we all make mistakes and these are better made as a young adult, when the consequences of spending and investing money are not too severe, and when the older generation is still around. Likewise, it's important to be able to talk about (and move past) these mistakes. And remember: it is not always just the younger generation who learns. Older members may learn valuable lessons about the younger, and about the art of giving.

Finally, there is the issue of 'too much love' – in other words, confusing being kind with being loving. Our children will always be our children. It is natural to feel responsible for them and to want to give them the best. And yet, with good intentions, we may spoil our children, ruin their sense of self and create a sense of dependency between parent and child. Being consistent, and occasionally being (empathically) tough, may be loving. Like the saying I learned from my mother: unless you cut the branches of the tree in spring, it will not bear fruit in summer.

6. The Purpose of Wealth Model – a practical planning tool
Control and flexibility. Ownership and trusteeship. In my experience, these are the central dimensions that a wealth owner must consider when creating their plan. Of course, we all have different appetites regarding control and flexibility. The Purpose of Wealth Model, which I will explain over the following pages, can help you to find yours and thus create a plan that better reflects your intentions in relation to different assets that will ultimately have a different planning purpose. As you can see in Figure 1, the model is built on two axes.

Figure 1. The Purpose of Wealth Model

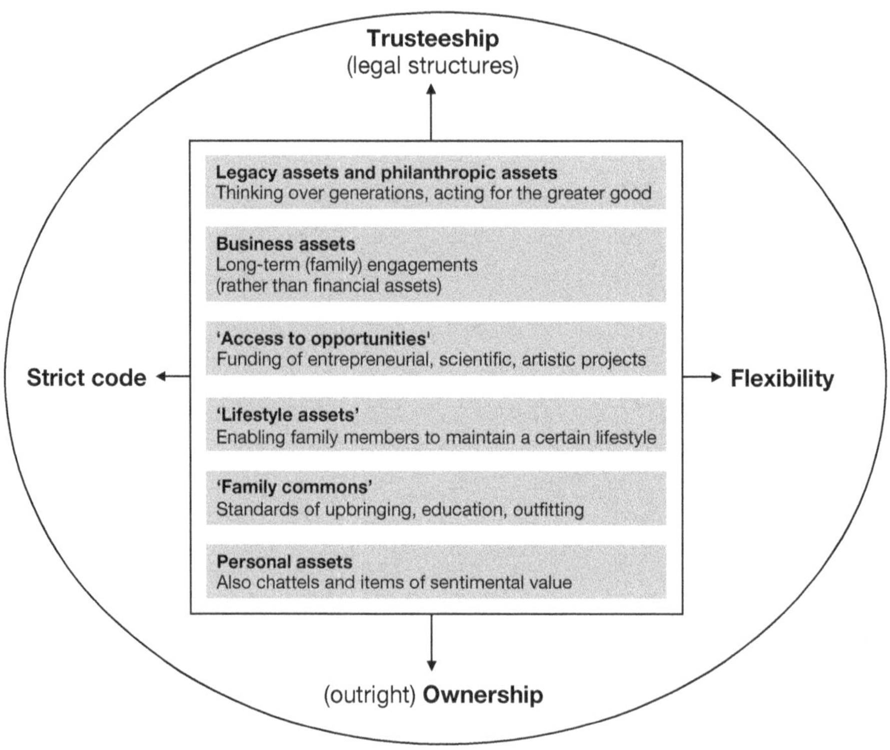

6.1 The first axis: trusteeship to outright ownership

Which assets are suited to be passed on outright and which are better preserved through legal instruments, such as corporate vehicles or trusts? It is essential to understand the difference.

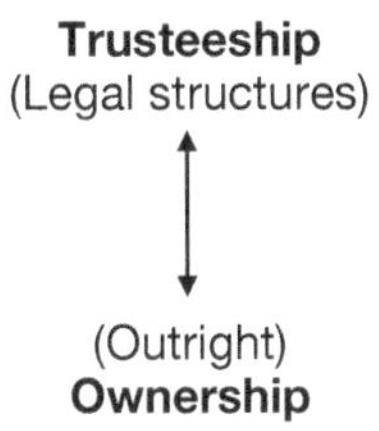

'Ownership' means that an individual can dispose of the asset as they see fit. They can use it, sell it – even destroy it.[15] Plus, ownership means that an asset becomes part of an individual's estate – and liable to be included in any divorce or bankruptcy proceedings.

Trusteeship, in contrast, legally separates assets from the settlor (ie, the person giving the assets) and the beneficiary (ie, the person receiving an entitlement to the assets). Instead of being owned by an individual, they are legally (but not economically, which I find myself sometimes hard to imagine) owned by a trustee or foundation, which can be 'programmed' to determine the exact purpose of the asset and its income, including how it is held, used and disposed of.

This not only enables the establishment of separate and independent estates for different branches of a family, but also creates legal continuity, which means that the arrangement can survive the original settlors or beneficiaries and mitigate potential conflicts among heirs. Just as importantly, it may help to ward off third-party claimants, such as spouses or creditors. Legal continuity can also protect minor children until they can themselves take ownership of the wealth.

Having a trustee hold wealth for individual successors (who may have very different needs and capabilities) also helps to avoid situations where responsibilities to look after interests and assets of certain family members are given to older (or, arguably, 'more capable') family members, often at the expense of their own freedom and wellbeing.

6.2 The option in between

However, there is an intermediate solution between ownership and trusteeship: assets may be held via partnerships or bodies corporate, such as holding companies, investment funds and other vehicles. The shares or ownership rights of such instruments enable shareholders to hold and dispose of their owner rights (subject to any contractual arrangements, such as shareholders' agreements, where pre-emptive rights, voting rights and dividend policies may be set in a binding way with all parties). However, shareholders cannot dispose of assets held by the vehicle in their capacity as shareholders unilaterally – for example, of a commercial property or business that will remain undivided.

The downside of such agreements is that individual shares remain in the ownership of the shareholders. Legal proceedings initiated against shareholders may affect their shares, expose other shareholders, potentially introduce undesirable shareholders or force existing shareholders to share information about the asset with non-family members. Moreover, because of the shares falling into the estates of the shareholders upon their death, there is a risk of fragmented shareholding over generations, which can render decision making difficult.

Against this background, many families decide to put a trust or foundation 'on top' of the shares, so that the trust holds the corporate entity and each branch of the family delegates a member to the advisory board of such a 'top' structure. This way, they can ensure that the family as a whole remains in charge.

6.3 The second axis: strict code and flexibility

The second axis reflects how much an asset (and its use) is determined by the instrument holding the asset; or how much freedom is built into the instrument for successors to change the initial arrangement.

Here is a simple example: a trust holding a bank account might provide that the annual income from the trust must be distributed to three beneficiaries every year; and that after 20 years the capital should be distributed in equal parts to the beneficiaries. This leaves no discretion to the trustee or the beneficiaries. The trust must remain the same throughout the 20 years. In other words, the settlor of the trust has full control over the destiny of the bank account.

Strict code ←——————→ **Flexibility**

However, the settlor can also encourage a more flexible approach. Let's say they want the assets' income to be available for beneficiary requests, such as school fees or medical care. Rather than a strict code, they can hand responsibility for these decisions over to the trustee, with guidance, by way of letter of wishes or similar instruments, on which requests are to be granted.

In this scenario, the settlor sets out the vision for the trust, but hands over control to the trustee (which is why proper guidance and suitable trustees are so important). And yet before you hand over control to a trustee, you should clearly define and potentially retain parts of the ultimate levers of decision making; because while there is no denying the usefulness of a trustee, you must give your close ones the necessary powers to ensure that the trustee is properly directed and supervised.

"While there is no denying the usefulness of a trustee, you must give your close ones the necessary powers to ensure that the trustee is properly directed and supervised."

6.4 Distinguish between ownership, control, income and use of an asset

In the context of the Purpose of Wealth Model, you may find that it is useful to look at the ownership, income and control of an asset separately. This is particularly important for families that hold a business. But it is also important for other tangible or liquid assets which require active, hands-on management — or for legacy assets which must be preserved, not divided, for future generations. After all, being able to benefit from an asset doesn't mean that you have to own it. Take a family home: you may be able to use it without owning it.

For this to work, you need:

- clear rules around usage, maintenance, administration and financing;
- clear rules on entitlement to income; and
- a mechanism to decide under which conditions the asset can be disposed of.

It is also useful to anticipate what types of disagreements and disputes might arise in this scenario – and to define a dispute resolution mechanism.

Obviously, an arrangement such as this depends on:

- the value system of the family;
- their notion of fairness; and
- the engagement and availability of talent.

On the one hand, you may want to create an entrepreneurial spirit and to reward people who contribute to the economic wellbeing of the family. On the other, you may want individuals to pursue their own talents; and non-economic contributions to the family may be highly desirable and valuable too. Then ultimately, why force someone into the world of business if their talent lies in the arts or medicine or science?

Creating a fair system for all these instances isn't always easy from a moral point of view. Plus, there are economic as well as legal restrictions to be considered if the value of a business or asset becomes too large relative to the other assets divided among heirs who benefit from forced heirship rights.[16]

6.5 How does your wealth work alongside the broader purpose of your plan?

When we look more specifically into the asset categories of the Purpose of Wealth Model, we realise that it is not always simple to

"There are economic as well as legal restrictions to be considered if the value of a business or asset becomes too large relative to the other assets divided among heirs who benefit from forced heirship rights."

decide whether the ownership or trustee approach works better for a particular asset. However, the general guidelines of the model have proven useful in developing a strategic, practical plan to structure wealth and succession, and elaborating it in detail. The categories enable wealth owners and families to define some of their core values, and enable the creation of different pots related to the giving and structuring of wealth – during life and in death. Unlike the traditional property law model, the categories also enable you to look at the *purpose and use* of each asset.

(a) Personal assets

These are assets (or 'chattels') that are intended for everyday use – and as such may not have huge significance in the overall value of an estate. And yet they can hold significant emotional value. Think of a necklace belonging to a mother or a wristwatch to a father. History is littered with examples of expensive, long-lasting family litigation because such items were 'lost' (or taken unilaterally by one of the heirs) after the passing of a parent. And so old patterns of envy are revived and trust is destroyed within the family.

In these scenarios, it is best to openly discuss the division of assets with sentimental value and either agree on allocation or define a fair mechanism to divide them (eg, by building various 'lots' from which heirs can draw).

(b) Lifestyle assets

These are the assets that enable individuals to lead a certain lifestyle – including liquidity for daily life (eg, travelling, paying taxes), and physical assets purchased for use and enjoyment. Some of these assets, such as real estate, may appreciate in value; others, such as ordinary cars, will depreciate. But whether they go up or down in value, they all cost money to maintain. That's why thinking about lifestyle assets entails several dimensions – particularly when planning for younger generations who may be used to a certain standard of living:

- How much should the younger generation be entitled to the same lifestyle after they leave the family home and live independently?
- How can you assure the long-term availability of assets to the younger generation?
- What conditions and incentives can you give the younger generation?
- Should they receive a regular income or capital; and if the latter, should the capital be protected (by way of a trust)?

Beneath these more practical questions is the issue of how you educate the younger generation to think about wealth. Do you want children to see money just as something they receive when they ask for it? Or do you want to agree with them on a regular allowance of size which encourages them to also 'own', not just 'spend', wealth, and reward if they are successfully saving?

How much to give, when and in what form, to neither spoil nor be too miserly?

Again, this isn't just about educating the younger generation; the older generation need to learn too. They need to learn to trust the younger generation, give them the freedom to spend their money and not overly control them through wealth. Likewise, the younger generation need to learn to limit themselves and be mindful in their spending – even if others (including parents) around them spend generously.

One well-proven solution is to give members of the younger generation a certain amount of capital, along with a mentor to help with the investment and administration of that capital. Importantly, it is best this mentor is not a parent – there are often too many personal or psychological issues to make this mentoring relationship with a parent a success. The mentor can guide the younger generation and report back to the parents with updates and achievements. Ideally, if the relationship works, the younger generation can live off the income from their investment (or at least partly), and learn what it means to have and accumulate wealth.

(c) Family commons

This relates closely to lifestyle assets, although is more basic. Family commons represent contributions to family members under special circumstances. They are particularly important if you intend a long-term legacy – or if you want to stipulate how your children are cared for in the event of your passing.

"MUM TOLD US TO CARRY OUR LEGACY FOR GENERATIONS TO COME"

For example, many families keep a certain amount of money in reserve for educational or medical purposes. This money will be held in a trust, shielded from the rest of the family wealth. There are also cases when a trust has been set up by a settlor with the purpose of enabling family members who get married to purchase real estate, so as not to become financially dependent on the spouse. Sometimes, these commons are even used to fund a defined minimum standard of living for future family members (usually based on average income or an index of their country of residence).

(d) Access to opportunities
Some families choose to create separate pots of wealth to help members pursue their own business ventures, charitable projects or other endeavours that may not be as financially rewarding as business. In terms of business ventures, you may hear of a fund such as this referred to as a 'family bank'.[17] On the one hand, it is a good way to encourage self-drive, entrepreneurship and a responsible attitude towards money. On the other hand, this approach of thinking more broadly about business and investment interests can help families to look more strategically into long-term wealth preservation; and to celebrate not only diversity of professional interests, but also diversification of their business and other assets.

This can be particularly true in scenarios where the shareholding of a multi-generational business is highly fractioned, without the opportunity for all branches of the family to actively participate in the business. In this case, a separate pot of wealth may help to maintain the entrepreneurial spirit in the family for generations to come. And it is a good way to help members who don't want to enter the family business – or who have other talents.

Usually, wealth owners define a process to analyse, evaluate and approve investment ideas and projects (and to decide whether they also want to participate in the venture by way of equity contributions or debt financing, or by granting options for the family to purchase the business in different circumstances, likely including first refusal rights and otherwise). Some families even decide to give members a 'one-off' gift of outright funding. The family may also specify ethical and moral conditions for ventures on the basis of religious, philosophical or environmental considerations; and it may be advisable to stipulate non-compete clauses, restricting the use of the family name and competition against the family's core businesses, to avoid conflicts.

Who is entitled to benefit and on what conditions?

(e) Business assets
The planning of business assets is half art, half science, and we may only scratch the surface here. Nonetheless, we can outline some of the most important questions you should consider:

- What is the role of the family business, now and in the future? Is it primarily to generate income for the family and future generations, or is it to foster an entrepreneurial legacy that brings the business in line with family culture?

- Who will take strategic decisions for, as well as within, the business (including a potential sale, for corporate finance and M&A or joint ventures)?
- Who should be a shareholder or partner in the business — all descendants or only those who take an active role? A trust or foundation?
- Who is entitled to benefit and on what conditions? Are dividends for all family members or only for those in the business?
- How are the shares held? Can family members dispose of shares if they wish? On what conditions? Or are they custodians for the next generations?
- What is the policy for the business: to distribute profits; to reinvest dividends in other family assets, such as a family venture fund or bank;[18] to diversify; or to donate to a charity?
- Who can enter the family business and on what terms? How will entry and exit be financed?
- How can you identify (objectively!), assess and develop talent for the future generations, as well as address weaknesses?

(f) Legacy assets

Legacy assets are assets for the generations to come – whether benefiting the family or a wider circle. Many entrepreneurs have turned their passion – be it collecting art or cars, looking after extraordinary real estate or developing their business – into a public good, such as a museum, natural reserve or heritage trust. And these public goods have benefited not just family members, but also employees, communities and charities.

Planning for these assets first requires a clear purpose. But the legacy assets also need to be legally separated from the rest of the family's wealth, so that a more tailored approach can be taken. And aside from legal separation, they need independent endowment, so that the legacy venture may become self-funding and can therefore be properly maintained.

(g) Setting up a charity

This is a transformative experience for a family, and I have often heard from wealth owners of the joy of sharing and making an impact. Likewise, philanthropy can strengthen relationships within the family and unite individuals around a common purpose. It allows family members from different generations, with different skills, to work and achieve together.

But there is an important first watch-out: many wealth owners underestimate the work involved in establishing a charity of their own. This is why it's so important to address the questions of scope: is the

"Moving beyond donations means that you can potentially have a greater impact – particularly in areas that are dear to you and underserved by other charities."

charity intended to support existing charities and activities through donations and other support? Or is the ambition wider: do you want to build an organisation that leads activities and mobilises others? The latter requires serious commitment to the strategy, management and governance of the charity (and how it is created). Funding existing charities can be more efficient and certainly takes less time. Of course, you still need to take time to find suitable partners (and conduct due diligence). However, moving beyond donations means that you can potentially have a greater impact – particularly in areas that are dear to you and underserved by other charities. This option can be more satisfying and allow for a more hands-on approach too.

The second area to consider is personal engagement. Like scope, this also throws up a range of questions: how involved do you want to be in the charity – including sitting on the board, hosting events, attending media interviews? How will other family members be involved? Compared with operating a business, philanthropy can allow a more diverse range of ages and talents to be combined. How much do you want outsiders engaged? Do you want your charitable activities to remain discreet and private, between a network of personal contacts? Or do you want them to become part of a wider movement, through which you collaborate with like-minded people from around the world?

7. Bringing it all together: your family constitution and governance

Now we are approaching the end of our discussion. As we have seen, within the issue of wealth and succession planning are myriad emotions, desires and considerations. The further you explore, the more questions you uncover. The more questions you ask, the more puzzle pieces you discover. Your family, your business, your investments: all of the pieces must fit together like a clockwork. How, then, should you wrap these questions into a single form? One possible answer is with a family constitution. Of course, this is not a novel suggestion. Many families have constitutions these days. Almost anybody can create one, after asking a few simple questions. You can even download template constitutions from the Internet. But for me, this is not a living constitution. First, because every family is unique and no off-the-shelf template can possibly match their complexities. Second, because a family constitution is more than just a document; it is a process – a process of continuously asking the right questions, validating solutions and putting those solutions into action.

Many families are proud to have created their own constitution, and rightly so: it is a significant achievement. However, it is just the beginning of the process, not the end. Once a constitution has been created, further work will be waiting; because in my experience, a family constitution truly works only if it combines a rigorous, well-thought-through plan with real, regular implementation.

> ***Creating a family constitution is the beginning of the process, not the end.***

7.1 The essentials of a family constitution

Nevertheless, first things first: what is a family constitution? Put simply, it is a document which formalises a family legacy. It governs the relationships between family members, the family business and its shareholders, investors, the family office (if there is a formal one), the family fiduciaries and corporate structures, as well as the allocation and governance of all investments, by defining the various roles, responsibilities and competences of the different organs, and by setting forth the checks and balances too. (That was a long sentence, and you may want to read it again and have a look at the anatomy of governance chart set out in Figure 2.) A family constitution helps to set a clear family vision, plus values, for the coming generations. It is not normally a legally binding document. Yet certain legal instruments, such as wills and nuptial agreements, may be used to implement the rules and principles outlined in the constitution.

Every family will take a different approach, but typically they will use a constitution to set the direction for the family over the next

Figure 2. Anatomy of governance chart

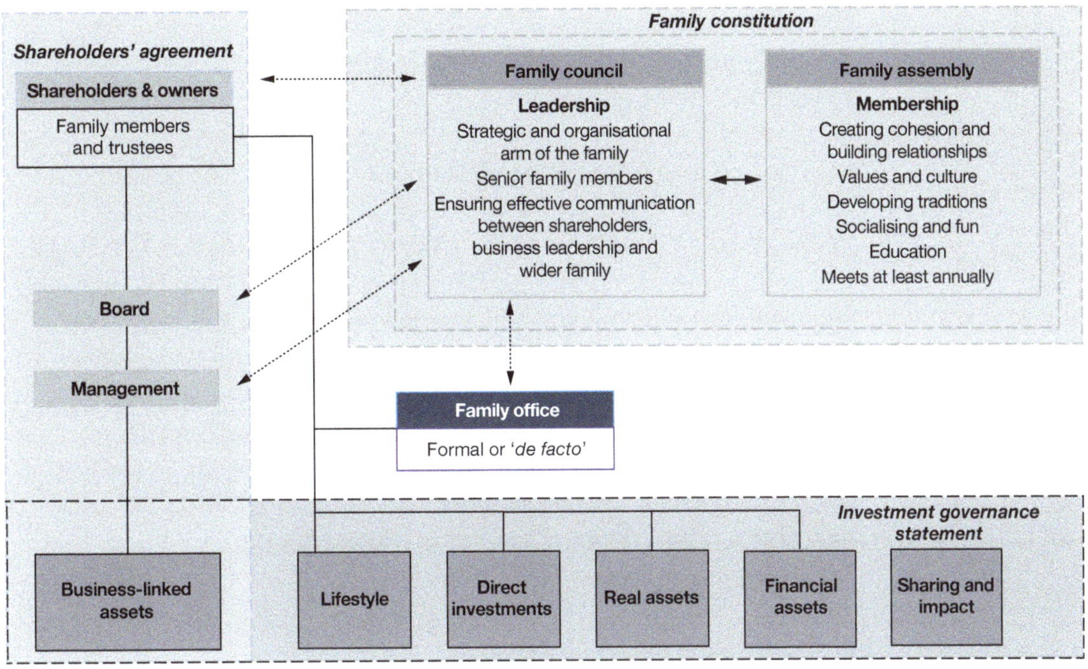

generations and to create a forum for communication that helps the family to remain connected as it grows over time. A constitution should contain a mechanism for dispute resolution, and for the education and mentoring of younger members. It also needs rules for decision making around family businesses, and in many cases the values that the family wants to formally embody across all aspects of their relationships and assets.

7.2 Making it happen

A good starting point for a constitution is a workshop with the family and their key advisers. In such a workshop, the goal is to establish the relevant facts and gain a clear picture of the priorities and objectives of each main member. Then you may begin to think about how your governance platform will affect how you do things today – including your business management. This will enable you to understand the changes that will need to be made for your constitution to be effective.

And next comes the hard part: implementing your constitution and keeping it alive. In my experience, this is the part of the process that is usually underestimated. To make it happen, roles and responsibilities may need to shift within the family. Some people may need to step up, while others take a back seat. This requires people to change their behaviour, which is easier said than done.

This is where family retreats can prove invaluable. These are regular family meetings for the family to review its wealth, business and philanthropic activities. But more than that, they are a chance to connect (and stay connected).[19] This is particularly important for growing international families, where a great deal of work is needed to keep the family aligned.

How do you oversee a successful family retreat? A good amount of strategic thinking and preparation is essential to make sure that members participate, contribute and enjoy the experience. This is also where an experienced, independent, trusted outsider can be invaluable – not only to help draft the constitution and agenda, but also to help implement it for generations to come. In any event, it is always useful to have someone independent on hand to look at the bigger picture, who can help to raise the difficult, fundamental questions that conserve the core of the existing traditions and bring about innovation. Because questions, ultimately, are at the heart of successful wealth planning. Asking the right ones – and finding the right people to help answer them – is essential.

8. Finally, on a personal note

"A few numbers change here and there, and thousands of workers erect a skyscraper. Some other numbers change, and a venerable business shuts its doors."[20] As an entrepreneur or wealth owner, you have it in your hands to take a lead on change. The challenges that we are facing as a species are many. They are not waiting for us, and we are the custodians of the future, which belongs to the next generations. I am humbled and grateful to have found my own call in helping individuals and families to define their purpose, and in shaping their wealth and governance to create meaningful relationships to achieve their goals. Wealth is a powerful means to an end. By using it responsibly, we make a difference. Building your wealth plan requires commitment and skills; but once your platform is in place, it will enable you and your loved ones to apply their talents and share their individual contributions towards creating "the more beautiful world our hearts tell us is possible".[21] I wish you the best of luck on your own journey.

Notes

1 Roberto Assagioli, *Transpersonal Development, Smiling Wisdom* (Findhorn, 2007), pp207 and 215.
2 Jaak Panksepp, *The Archaeology of Mind: Neuroevolutionary Origins of Human Emotions* (Norton & Company, 2012), p3.
3 Michael Lowe, "Drexel University on Hedonic Hunger", *Scientific American – Neuroscience*, January 2016.
4 For more insights on the psychology of wealth from the perspective of different members of the family (including wealth creators to their partners and descendants), see Philip Marcovici, *The Destructive Power of Wealth* (John Wiley & Sons Ltd, 2016), pp19–43.
5 Panksepp (n 2), p5.
6 Despite all our fears, concerns (and potential envies over other people having more!), the fundamental, unavoidable question remains, for each one of us to answer: how much is, in the end,

enough? In this respect, an interesting formula is the 'Da Vinci Constraint' of Ricardo Semler, applying Leonardo da Vinci's "*De Divina Proportione*" illustration to a theory about having enough wealth. Ricardo Semler, *The Seven-Day Weekend* (Random House Business, 2004), pp103–106.
7 Irvin D Yalom, *Existential Psychotherapy* (Basic Books, 1980).
8 From working with families, I normally find striking what amount of wisdom, enriching perspectives and knowledge the younger generation bring into the discussions. I will never forget a teenage third-generation wealth owner at a large family gathering saying: "Our family would be different if we used the two phrases 'I love you' and 'I'm sorry' more often." For further inspirations, see Piero Ferruci, *What Our Children Teach Us: Lessons in Joy, Love, and Awareness* (Warner Books, 2001).
9 'Affluenza' is a psychological malaise supposedly affecting wealthy young people, symptoms of which include a lack of motivation, feelings of guilt and a sense of isolation (*Oxford Dictionaries*).
10 I recall the lesson of Baron Eric de Rothschild who, when asked how his family had successfully transitioned wealth through many generations, replied: "I cannot tell you exactly, but here is my advice. First, love your children. Second, stay close to them and gain their trust. And third, give them the right responsibilities from early on."
11 See Iraj Ispahani's chapter in this Special Report: "Managing your context today and finding and deploying purpose".
12 Viktor E Frankl, *The Will to Meaning* (Plume/Penguin, 2014), p43.
13 For more insights on this topic, read Joline Godfrey, *Raising Financially Fit Kids* (Ten Speed Press, Revised Edition, 2013).
14 A useful exercise: imagine you favoured one child over the other (eg, with a significantly larger share in your assets). Now fast-forward to the time after you: how do you think the quality of the relationship between the two siblings would be?
15 Consider the example of Sandra West, a wealthy LA socialite, who in 1977 was buried in her beloved Ferrari 330. It was, as the funeral director said at the time, "the most unusual" funeral he had ever managed – and yet Mrs West was entirely within her rights to make it happen.
16 See below sections 6.5(d) and (e).
17 See Ed Lee's chapter in this Special Report: "The family bank: creating the next generation of entrepreneurs". See also: Ed Lee, Philip Marcovici and Stefan Liniger, "Family businesses and the increasing importance of the family bank" (September 2020), www.ispahaniadvisory.com/publications.
18 See above at (d).
19 Philip Marcovici, (n 4), p131.
20 Charles Eisenstein, *Sacred Economics* (North Atlantic Books, 2011), p143.
21 *Ibid*, p437.

VII. The family bank: creating the next generation of entrepreneurs

Ed Lee
Bowbridge

1. Introduction

One of the great ironies in many eminent families is that the entrepreneurial flair that was present in the generation that created the wealth is often much-dampened in the next generation and beyond. There is little logic to it; intuitively, the next generation has a great platform to thrive from, with the benefit of learning from their highly successful parents/grandparents and starting from a significant position of wealth. So why do so many second and third-generation wealth owners struggle to find the magic dust that their predecessors had and used to such great effect?

While creativity and flair are undoubtedly important factors, the making of a successful entrepreneur is often derived from a blend of passion, resilience and discipline – a concept encapsulated by Thomas Edison, who described genius as "1% inspiration and 99% perspiration".[1] Another attribute often seen in first-generation wealth creators is the presence of a 'nothing to lose' mentality. One of the great entrepreneurs of the 20th century, Walt Disney, filed for bankruptcy in 1921 at the age of just 20 after a failed first foray into business. Indeed, he had several false starts in his early career before finding the magic formula for success in the 1930s. By his death in the 1960s, he had amassed a fortune of $5 billion – the equivalent of $42 billion in today's terms. His relentless pursuit of his dreams and resilience in the face of repeated setbacks were the secret to his ultimate success, and the same mentality is evident in many of the most eminent entrepreneurs in the world today.

Intuitively, if you combine innate genetic flair with significant inherited wealth, it would be reasonable to expect the next generation to naturally be in a position to build upon the platform they receive and take it to the next level of success. However, that is rarely the case. More often than not, it is because of an inhibiting fear of failure – the fear of eroding the value that previous generations had worked so hard to build. This can naturally create a cautious mindset focused on preservation rather than growth; and in doing so, there is a danger that generations become passive custodians of wealth rather than active creators. It is also undoubtedly harder to instil the same level of drive and ambition in a generation that has grown up surrounded by the benefits of the wealth created by previous generations.

With significant inheritance tax burdens in most jurisdictions and the natural dilution of wealth through generations, this mindset of inactive preservation is a major danger to wealth-owning families around the world. The implications are severe and the challenges of maintaining and growing wealth through the generations are widely recognised: research from the Williams Group shows that as many as 70% of wealthy families lose their wealth by the second generation, rising to 90% by the third generation.[2]

Beyond the lack of positive impact of wealth ownership, there are also many stories of families where inheriting wealth has had an actively negative impact on individuals and their mental health, as Dr Paul Hokemeyer capably addresses in Chapter IV.

The single most powerful way to address all of these challenges is by creating purpose, and it is vital that each family member finds theirs – in whichever field that may be.

2. The challenges of multi-generational wealth preservation

If the saying "Money makes money" is true, then why is it so difficult for so many families to protect and enhance wealth? Many factors are external ones that are, to a certain degree, beyond the control of families. However, there are also many internal factors which are eminently more avoidable – dispute, disaffection, divorce, dysfunction and death, to name a few. Much of the secret to multi-generational success lies in minimising issues where matters are in their control, and positioning the people and financial interests within the family to best withstand external factors that are not.

The most vulnerable time for families is widely recognised as the point of succession. Invariably, families try to walk a tightrope between encouraging the next generation to get involved in the family business and giving them free rein to make their own decisions and make their own way, meaning that succession planning is rarely as comprehensive as it should be. It is also a complex issue that is hard to comprehensively address and procrastination on the subject is thus very common. The result is that strategic dialogue between the generations is often very limited at the critical age of 18 to 25 and, accordingly, not enough thought goes into how to build the skills that the individual and the business operations need or will need in the future.

This doesn't happen because of lack of interest or engagement from either generation; families don't feel comfortable having these conversations because they somehow feel too prescriptive at an age when the next generation should be learning, questioning and exploring in equal measure, unstifled by the heavy weight of family duty. A balance must be struck between planning for the needs of the family's business interests and empowering the younger generation to plot their own chart. The senior generation are therefore reluctant to force the conversation of succession and the younger generation are understandably reticent to push for inclusion, preferring to 'wait for

"Much of the secret to multi-generational success lies in minimising issues where matters are in their control, and positioning the people and financial interests within the family to best withstand external factors that are not."

the call-up'. It is no surprise, therefore, that this delays the dialogue and leads to deficiencies in strategic direction, leadership and decision making at a critical time.

Through no fault of their own, this means the next generation are often simply not ready for the handover. This is backed up by the statistics: as many as one in three family offices have no plans for a change in control despite the majority being led by people in their 60s and 70s, according to the 2020 Global Family Office Report from UBS.[3] When combined with the less avoidable succession challenges of dilution of ownership, potential syndication of decision making and wider market factors, it is imperative that families create an environment with open dialogue and encouragement for all relevant family members to make a positive impact from an early stage.

The instigation of succession-related conversations has naturally traditionally been at the discretion of the senior generation because they oversee family operations and succession happens only when they are ready to cede control to their successors. The next generation do not feel that it is their place to initiate such conversations, for fear of appearing grasping or presumptuous. It is then left to the incumbent generation to determine the appropriate moment to

"Finding a successor is one of the biggest determining factors of the success of a career. Without a succession plan, a lot of hard work and success can be undone."

open the dialogue; and all too often that is done when the elder generation are beginning to think about retiring, rather than 10 to 15 or more years in advance, which is often the sort of time period needed to effect a smooth and structured transition.

The consequence is that it becomes a half-handover, with the senior generation unable to step back with confidence and the younger generation inhibited by a sense of unreadiness. Combining this with the likely perception of nepotism among the non-family management team, it is therefore little wonder that it becomes harder and harder for the next generation to successfully step up; and this all stems from poor planning and communication.

Finding a successor is one of the biggest determining factors of the success of a career. Without a succession plan, a lot of hard work and success can be undone; and while responsibility for delivering successful generation change does rest principally with the senior generation, if approached sensitively to the specific scenario, the younger generation can proactively instigate the dialogue and positively effect change.

The potential benefits of such proactivity are considerably wider than simply ensuring that succession conversations are initiated sufficiently in advance of succession itself. The incoming generation are also often in a position of strength, in that they can look more objectively at the overall family operations and consider the portfolio of holdings in the context of ever-changing external factors. Innovation and adaptability to changing circumstances are crucial in facilitating longevity, and the next generation are often better equipped to understand the implications than their predecessors. Beyond the external factors, there are also changes in priorities through the generations. Sustainability is an ever-increasing priority, particularly for the Millennial and Generation Z age groups, as world-leading impact investment specialist Jed Emerson discusses in Chapter VIII of this Special Report. The emergence of responsible, sustainable and impact investing in recent years highlights the changes in priorities beyond simply wealth creation, with families increasingly thinking about the 'bottom line' being measured on social and environmental factors, as well as the traditional financial factors. What is also becoming increasingly apparent is that environmental, social and governance (ESG) related matters need not necessarily be to the detriment of financial returns.

According to the 2020 UBS Global Family Office Report, 39% of family offices intend to allocate most of their portfolios sustainably in five years' time, which is a quite staggering shift.[4] The next generation are more determined than any that went before them that wealth should be used as a force for good; and this is not something that should be addressed in a binary way at, or soon after, succession. It needs to be done in a systematic and structured way by both generations working in unison, striking a balance between respecting the senior generation's plans and legacy while ensuring that family operations are best placed to deliver desired outcomes in changing times.

Simply having these discussions between the generations provides a more open line of communication and increases the likelihood of developing a coherent and integrated longer-term strategy. If the next generation are more reticent to step forward until invited to do so, it can have damaging effects on the long-term future of the family holdings; and it is the responsibility of both generations to foster proactivity and entrepreneurial attitudes so that the next generation can be in the best position to step up successfully.

3. Why is it important to develop entrepreneurial attitudes?
While ESG can sometimes be well addressed within trading businesses, it is usually the case that a greater focus on such matters means a requirement to further diversify away from a single trading business. In doing so, this can provide a much broader spectrum of opportunities to find a role for the next generation that marries increasing responsibility within the family with likely closer proximity to the interests and skills most suited to individual family members.

While ESG and sustainability are increasingly important, they are just two of many factors that benefit from a broader perspective. Aside from these attitudinal changes, just about every sector is more susceptible to disruption than it has ever been before – whether it's from a technological, economic, political or social perspective – and the need for diversification has never been greater than it is today. This is particularly exacerbated by the digital revolution – and not just the amount of change, but the speed of it. According to research by Family Capital, 55% of all family offices still own the original family business and 47% are still in the first generation.[5] Many such families have 80% to 90% of their interests in one business, which creates reliance on a single trading vehicle and serious ramifications for the business and family members if it encounters difficulties. Nowhere has this been illustrated better than through the devastating effect that the COVID-19 pandemic has had on so many sectors. Aside from that uniquely damaging and largely unforeseeable event, there are many examples of businesses and sectors in recent years that have failed to innovate or diversify and have paid the consequence. Fostering an entrepreneurial mindset in the next generation can be an important element of broadening horizons to capitalise on opportunities and mitigate issues. While innumerable internal and external pressures can arise, one thing is clear: in order to address them, families increasingly need to think outside of their main trading and investment operations and undertake more comprehensive long-term strategic planning across the entirety of family interests.

A key decision that families need to make is whether each individual in the next generation will join the family business and, if so, at what stage in their careers they should do so. Joining straight after school or university intuitively gives the best platform to start building knowledge and understanding of the business, but that forgoes the valuable breadth of perspectives and skills that can be developed elsewhere. On top of this, within family businesses there is all too regularly the danger that the next generation will be in the shadow of the elder generation, compared unfairly to the wealth creators too early in their careers and naturally dismissed as a pale imitation of the patriarch or matriarch. Encouraging the next generation to plough their own furrow outside of the core business does not mean that there won't be an appropriate time in the future to join the fray. Indeed, gaining lived experience in other businesses, sectors or regions means that family members can join the business further down the line, armed with a broader business perspective that can benefit all of the family's business interests and not just the core trading entity. It also doesn't need to be binary; the next generation should be encouraged to be engaged with family operations from an early age, even if their main role is elsewhere for some or all of their careers.

"Gaining lived experience in other businesses, sectors or regions means that family members can join the business further down the line, armed with a broader business perspective that can benefit all of the family's business interests."

An important benefit of gaining wider experience is that it helps people to think more dispassionately about business and investment interests, and have a broader mindset than simply 'the business'. Given the ever-accelerating rate of global change, many families need to make tough decisions on the focus of the family's business interests, and people naturally find this a difficult thing to do – whether it's a successful entrepreneur who has built their 'baby' from scratch or a business that has been in the family for many generations with deeply ingrained tradition and history. The challenge is to ensure that emotional ties to the business do not inhibit good decision making. Broader lived experiences help families to strategically diversify, innovate and adapt to the benefit of current and future generations, and facilitate less subjective decision making.

4. Fostering entrepreneurialism: the family bank concept
Businesses that survive and thrive over generations are those that adapt to changing times and take advantage of opportunities that arise. Preparing family members for the wide range of ways in which they can enhance a family business or portfolio of investments can be an exciting way to develop and capture diverse talents within the family.

A simple example: a family may be transitioning to the third generation of ownership of a meaningful family business. Like most wealth-owning families, work is done on developing continuity and governance frameworks designed to protect the family business and to ensure effective family oversight, perhaps as non-operating owners of the family business. But how much work is done by the family to encourage and support the diverse interests of the younger generation? Is there clarity regarding how the family might support and capture the entrepreneurial endeavours of the younger generation? If there is no discussion and clarity on these issues, what happens when a child approaches their parents with a business idea that might be worthy of support? If the parents decide to make funds available for the business venture, who enjoys the success of the investment if the business does well? Who suffers if the business fails? The other children in the family may be resentful if their sibling is supported in an investment that then produces great success for that sibling, given the family investment involved. If the business fails and the funds are lost, the reduction in the wealth of the parents will affect all the siblings, and not only the one involved in the investment.

A better way is sometimes for the family to develop a 'family bank' mindset. Whether done formally or informally, the main objective is for the family to discuss and agree an approach to be taken both to encourage and to support entrepreneurial activity in the younger generation. And where appropriate, there could be a formula that might allow for such entrepreneurial activity to be retained or shared by the family. The approaches that a family might consider addressing include the following:

- Funds are set aside and made available to support entrepreneurial activities in the younger generation.
- An approach to evaluating investment possibilities is developed and agreed. This might involve links to third-party valuers and business consultants to help guide investment decisions.
- A family member with a business idea presents the idea to the 'family bank'. If an investment is to be made, it follows an agreed approach; this might, for example, involve the family bank's investment taking the form of debt and equity – say, 80% being in the form of debt, carrying an agreed rate of interest, and 20% being equity. If the investment made by the family member promoting the project is successful, the family bank owns a 20% interest in the business and will be repaid the 80% debt. If it is unsuccessful, the family bank has lost its 20% equity investment, but the debt portion is taken out of the relevant family member's future share in family succession. The percentages and approach matter less than coming to a clear understanding within the family, in advance, on how the family bank might work. In order to 'capture' the business for the long-term endeavours of the family as a whole, the investment by the family bank might carry with it options for the family to purchase the business in different circumstances, including likely first refusal rights and otherwise.

There are many different structures that a family bank can take – it is often a trust set up for the beneficiaries with trustees overseeing its operations. Other structures include family limited partnerships, foundations or limited family investment companies with alphabet shares. It is also often valuable for families to have more than one structure in place. There are even ownerless structures, such as the Liechtenstein-based Interogo Foundation, which was set up by the Kamprad family, the owners of Ikea. With the stated purpose of "secur[ing] the independence and longevity of the IKEA Concept", it is a self-owned entity which has no individual beneficiary.[6] Funds held by the foundation can be used only in accordance with the foundation's purpose, providing a vision that delivers focus and clarity to all stakeholders. The Interogo Foundation is one that has a public profile, which might be the right solution for some families; others prefer a more discreet approach. There is no single structure that will work for all families – each will have a different solution that works for them. These concepts are of relevance to families with simpler and lower amounts of wealth, as well as to the more complex situations of families at the higher end of wealth. The family bank can also address very simple concepts, such as how to fund university and other education of family members in a fair way.

Such an approach can foster a valuable entrepreneurial spirit in the next generation, who can benefit from intra-family financing while also receiving a crucial support framework. If the next generation has clarity on the structures in place for the different potential paths they may follow, this increases the likelihood that they will make good decisions for themselves and their role in the family, in terms of both higher education and early career choices. It also facilitates a healthier, more timely and more comprehensive conversation between the generations about individual plans and the needs of business operations. There will always be the element which is reliant on open dialogue between family members; but having the structures in place to facilitate those conversations and provide clarity to all parties will give the highest likelihood of success.

5. How to engage the next generation
According to Deloitte's Family Office Symposium delegate survey, when asked about the most important and strategic challenge that faced the family, educating and motivating the next generation was the most critical issue for respondents, alongside the continued

Figure 1. What do you feel is the most important and strategic challenge facing the family you serve?

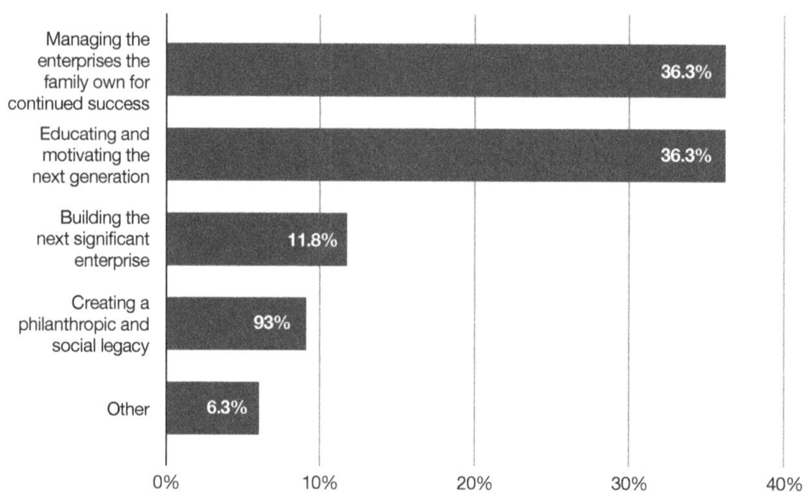

Source: Adapted from data from the Deloitte 2018 Family Office Symposium delegate survey.

success of the family business.[7] This highlights quite how crucial and challenging an issue it is for families, and demonstrates how much time needs to be devoted to achieving it.

One of the main reasons why so many families struggle to engage the next generation is that they have traditionally placed most emphasis on how best to fit family members into the main trading enterprises. This approach is starting to change, with increasing numbers of families instead focusing on tailoring family operations to best utilise the specific skills and interests of the individuals. In most cases, this is part of a wider diversification strategy, and it is important in understanding and serving changing priorities through the generations.

Aside from the evolving focuses, it is highly unlikely that the market conditions, technology, business environment and innate individual skills/interests that made the previous generation(s) successful will be the same as those that make the next generation successful. Innovation is critical, and this can be done either within or outside of the main trading business.

Taking an individual-led approach can facilitate diversified growth, but it also benefits the individuals themselves by giving them purpose and clarity. Human and financial capital are symbiotic, and providing family members with the opportunity to form and apply their own skills and passions is an important step in building engagement. Private investments are an ever-increasing focus of asset allocation and, according to the 2020 UBS Global Family Office Report, 69% of family offices now view private investments as a key driver of returns.[8] A large part of this is due to the changing focuses of the next generation and an acknowledgement that such diversification is required in order to deliver a platform for balanced and sustainable growth. There are a number of different models that this might take and each case is different. Some family members may want to pursue a specific opportunity, while others may want to build a portfolio of business interests.

A good example of a family encouraging the rising next generation to find purpose and pursue diversification is the Rausing family. The dynasty was forged by Ruben Rausing, who founded Tetra Pak in the early 20th century, and has gone from strength to strength through the subsequent generations. Jörn Rausing's son Magnus represents the fourth generation and has established a venture capital business backed by family capital, from which he has built a significant and growing portfolio of over 30 venture investments across multiple sectors that stand to generate strong and diversified returns.

The most crucial component in a successful and harmonious family operation is clarity for all parties – clarity of purpose, of strategy, of structure and of boundaries – and the way to achieve this is through a clear and communicable purpose that is understood by each relevant party. Legally documenting such matters can all too easily become overcomplicated for the people defining them, let alone subsequent generations trying to interpret them, and can thus defeat their very purpose. There is a fine balance between comprehensive structuring and clarity of message. A family constitution is not something that gets signed, filed and forgotten about; it is something that needs to be lived and breathed by all the people and businesses it seeks to protect and enhance.

6. What can the next generation do?

Passion and drive are important characteristics of wealth creators – in particular, those who are 'self-made'. It can be hard for the next generation to replicate that drive to the same degree, having benefited from the wealth that their predecessors have created. It is particularly difficult because these attributes are intangible – entrepreneurship is something of an enigmatic concept that is difficult to define and even harder to teach.

"Aside from the undoubted technical skill that an MBA can provide, the breadth of participants provides each cohort with a lifelong network of valuable relationships."

In the academic world, there is much debate as to appropriate teaching methods that can develop entrepreneurial capabilities which, in itself, is symptomatic of how difficult it is to understand. One theme has emerged from the many studies that have taken place: practical, lived experience is more beneficial than classroom or lecture-based learning.

The lack of obvious avenues to develop business insight in the education system places more emphasis on early career decisions. As a result, master of business administration (MBA) courses remain a popular choice among next generation family members for learning a blend of commerce and management in a neutral and external environment; and aside from the undoubted technical skill that an MBA can provide, the breadth of participants provides each cohort with a lifelong network of valuable relationships.

Despite the breadth of opportunities to develop skills, the most important attributes that are needed in the next generation are best learned by example: work ethic, discipline and the confidence to take calculated risks and own decisions. These are traits that can be developed from an early age by the incumbent generation – leading by example; teaching the next generation the value of money; taking the time to discuss and engage on business matters; encouraging participation and dialogue. One of the unfortunate hazards of wealth is the risk that inheritors drift through life without any drive or work ethic, lacking the 'need to succeed'. There is the example of the eminent European family that sold a hugely valuable trading business in the early 1900s and established a trust for family members. Now, 100 years later, only one of the 35 inherited beneficiaries of the trust is actively in work and the once-vast wealth continues to dwindle. Within two more generations, the legacy will be gone.

Regardless of the scale of wealth, the concept of needing to earn one's involvement should be present in all families and is to the ultimate benefit of the next generation in the long run. There are few more damaging things than the next generation becoming accustomed to dividend streams before they understand the value of money. In the most successful family offices that I deal with, one common attribute that the incoming generations share is a similar mindset that combines entrepreneurial drive with a blend of responsibility, humility and level-headedness with money. Those who are best positioned to thrive are usually those who have the mentality of being the custodian of wealth rather than the owner of wealth, with a recognition that success should broadly be measured in terms of passing on more to the next generation (in real terms) than was received. This mindset promotes varied positive behaviours: in a business sense, it fosters engagement, purpose and ambition; and in a human sense, it breeds modesty, maturity and stability.

"Family offices are often under-advised at the highest level: where the strategy is formed and implemented."

The senior generation sets the tone, with successors innately likely to follow the example that has been set to them. While not universally so, in my experience, those who carry themselves in an understated manner are usually those who instil the right behaviours in their successors and provide the strongest platform to transition wealth and happiness through the generations.

Typically, the harder part of the blend is the entrepreneurial element. It is a widely held belief that people are either entrepreneurial or they are not – as if this is a binary thing; but encouraging engagement in conversations and ideas on business matters undoubtedly helps to foster intuitive entrepreneurial thinking.

Once family members are of an age to begin thinking about higher education and their early careers, it is important to try to develop an understanding of what potential opportunities there may be in the future, whether within a trading business, elsewhere in the family office or outside of the family operations. Seeking clarity on the types of opportunities that may be available will help to refine key decisions in those formative years from 18 to 25. Many of those decisions will have direct and indirect consequences on the years that follow, so it is important to ensure that they are made with as informed a judgement as possible.

Succession is a team game, and the proactivity of the next generation is a vitally important role within it. Within the full breadth of family operations, there is invariably a sizeable knowledge base from which to learn and grow; and having the confidence to seek guidance and insight is valuable, whether that is directly from family members or from non-family employees or advisers. Outside of family operations, it is also helpful to seek the perspectives of other families and how they are addressing issues and fostering innovation. Advice – both formal and informal – is important to all people of all ages and stages of experience, but is particularly important for those in the formative stages of their careers.

While there are usually advisers who fulfil specific remits (eg, lawyers, tax advisers, asset managers, key management), family offices are often under-advised at the highest level: where the strategy is formed and implemented. In many cases, it is not just hard to know the answers to issues and opportunities; it is hard to identify the issues and opportunities themselves.

Case study

I sat down with a fourth-generation member of one of the United Kingdom's largest privately held construction companies and discussed his experiences inside and outside of the family business.

Tell us about what you do and how it fits with the family business.

I sit on the main board for our group of companies, which comprises 13 businesses across several verticals in the United Kingdom and the United States. I chair our house building business and I am a director of the investment/development business. I have overseen significant growth on both sides, which has provided improved diversification and balance across our business interests.

I work closely with my brother and cousin, who have different specialisms from me. This was partly by design and partly good fortune. I also have a portfolio of private equity investments, where I have deployed family capital to support and grow exciting young businesses.

How has your family helped you to establish your position?

My family have been hugely supportive and have struck a great balance between providing support and encouraging me to make my own mistakes. There has always been an open dialogue and an encouragement to pursue the career I wanted to pursue, and to join the business when I was ready to do so. I was always going to join the family business at some stage, and so my higher education choices were shaped by that. Looking back, it was extremely helpful for me to have clarity from an early age that I was wanted in the family business as soon as I was ready. It was also very helpful that my father wasn't too prescriptive about what my role would entail, enabling me to find my own path.

In my early career, I trained as a chartered surveyor with a leading firm and I subsequently spent several years as a director of a property development company, all the while staying close to what was happening with the family business. I then joined the family fold as an employee, gaining experience through the ranks to ready myself to join the group board, which I did a few years ago.

How have you developed your entrepreneurial skills and how do you think this will benefit you and the wider family now and in the future?

Having the freedom to find my own way has helped me to build skills and forge a career that I really enjoy. I worked away from the business for 10 years, learning and absorbing as much as I could along the way. It has been incredibly valuable to get external experience and perspective on business operations. In turn, this has meant that I am better placed to be enterprising and to ensure that the family business continues to evolve its operations.

Outside of the family business, I am a non-executive director across a series of smaller companies in a variety of sectors. This breadth of exposure is helpful for me to see how people are innovating across many different spheres. I also chair a charity that provides funding to smaller UK-based charities doing dynamic work with young people.

What are the biggest challenges that you have faced in stepping up into the family operations?

There are four things that stand out to me:

- *People assuming that you know everything;*
- *People not challenging you (except at the most senior level);*
- *Managing risk/avoiding failure; and*
- *The difficulty of failing publicly.*

What advice would you give other next generation members looking to find engagement and purpose?

Experience life away from your family business before you enter and bring something to the table on that basis. With it comes the confidence that you're there on merit, which does wonders for self-worth and engagement. My charitable work is a real passion as well, with a great sense of purpose and desire to make a positive contribution to our communities – a mindset that is shared by all of our family members. Aside from the direct impact that we are making and the satisfaction that gives us, it also helps to nurture a special values-led ethos across our companies. In my mind, it's no coincidence that so many of our clients keep coming back to us.

7. Closing thoughts

There are many positive and negative emotions that come with inherited wealth. On the one hand, individuals feel fortunate and stable; but on the other hand, many feel the weight of pressure, a level of inadequacy or a lack of direction. Every eminent family has, to some degree, experienced challenges with individual family members, and these can cause immense difficulty from both personal and business perspectives.

By encouraging entrepreneurial pursuits, families can protect financial interests and provide purpose, infrastructure and support for all family members, giving them the best opportunity to positively engage and

"By encouraging entrepreneurial pursuits, families can protect financial interests and provide purpose, infrastructure and support for all family members."

thrive. In the words of Jeff Bezos: "One of the huge mistakes people make is that they try to force an interest on themselves. You don't choose your passions; your passions choose you."[9] Families need to be flexible, agile and open-minded to new ideas and opportunities.

The engagement of human capital is inextricably correlated with the performance of financial capital, and having the structure in place to provide both support and challenge to each member of the family is symbiotic in delivering financial success. It is increasingly important to take an integrated view of health and wealth in family organisations, and the entrepreneurial spirit that such an ethos can generate can help family members to thrive collectively and individually.

It is the joint responsibility of each generation to form and evolve a strategy and way of working that puts the family in the best position to identify and capitalise on the many opportunities and navigate the many challenges that come its way. The measure of success is not about who created the original fortune; the responsibility for every generation is to pass on a better platform to their children than they inherited themselves.

The secret for the next generation is ensuring that they build all of the credentials that will ultimately enable them to seamlessly step up. Most of these skills are from a behavioural perspective, and those who can be engaged, responsible, humble and hardworking – and confident as a result – will be the ones who give their families the best chance of thriving for generations to come.

Notes

1 James D Newton, *Uncommon Friends: Life with Thomas Edison, Henry Ford, Harvey Firestone, Alexis Carrel and Charles Lindbergh* (Mariner Books, 1989), p24.
2 Chris Taylor, "A little honesty might preserve the family fortune", Reuters (28 June 2016), www.reuters.com/article/us-money-generations-strategies-idUSKBN0OX1RH20150617.
3 UBS, *Global Family Office Report 2020*, www.ubs.com/global/en/global-family-office/reports/global-family-office-report-2020.html, p28.
4 *Ibid*, p4.
5 Institute of Family Business at WHU, "Viewpoint: The entrepreneurial spirit of Single Family Offices – old meets new economy", *Family Capital* (13 November 2018), www.famcap.com/2018/11/viewpoint-the-entrepreneurial-spirit-of-single-family-offices-old-meets-new-economy/.
6 Interogo Foundation, owner of IKEA Group, www.inter.ikea.com/en/this-is-inter-ikea-group/our-owner—interogo-foundation#:~:text=Interogo%20Foundation's%20main%20purpose%20is,were%20to%20face%20serious%20challenges.
7 Deloitte 2018 Family Office Symposium delegate survey; see Deloitte, "2019 Family Office Trends: What's next for single family offices?", www2.deloitte.com/content/dam/Deloitte/uk/Documents/private-markets/deloitte-uk-2019-family-office-trends.pdf, p2.
8 UBS (n 3) p5.
9 "Success and entrepreneurship: The ultimate list of inspirational quotes", StartupIstanbul, https://startupistanbul.com/blog/2015/04/success-and-entrepreneurship-the-ultimate-list-of-inspirational-quotes/.

VIII. The purpose of capital: exploring our relationship with money and meaning

Jed Emerson
Tiedemann Advisors

1. Wealth has weight

While those without significant financial resources may have fantasies of wealth as bringing liberation from material concerns, as enabling one to become light as a feather and free to live the good life (and yes, there are real upsides to having wealth!), in truth, significant wealth can also bring with it a significant burden.

Those who create great wealth often find that the mindset, practices and perspectives which enabled them to gather that wealth may not be as useful in moving from material success to deeper, real significance. True, some may understand the values of professional integrity and how to turn challenges into solutions as core business practices that contribute to wealth, and may have value elsewhere in life. Or they may know that in many ways, profit is simply the by-product of creating value for others – customers, investors, even corporate teams; and that an obsession with the financial bottom line alone may leave one with short-term profits, but perhaps having sacrificed long-term value.

Other creators of wealth find that turning from how to make it to the challenge of how to manage, invest, steward and pass on wealth comes with a host of new pressures and considerations that may feel quite burdensome. Late at night (when we are being fully honest with ourselves), we reflect on a new set of questions: "How will wealth distort my life? How will it affect my children's lives – indeed, how has the process of creating wealth already affected their lives? How have my responsibilities and relationships been altered or changed as a result of my success?"

On the other hand, those in the rising next generation who inherit significant wealth must sit with a different set of reflections: "Do I deserve the wealth with which I have been entrusted? Why did I win the genetic lottery and not any number of others that I see in the course of a day? How will I know whether I have been a good steward of that wealth? Can I confide in those who promote themselves as experts and advisers, or must I myself become an expert in wealth management? Can I trust the motivation of any of those I meet who are not also of my level of wealth? Or why do others assume that simply because I do have such wealth, I have anything in common with other high-net-worth individuals? And what happens if this wealth is lost on my watch – what if I become my family's proof of the common observation that families of wealth go from 'shirtsleeves to shirtsleeves in three generations'?"

The world is full of advice on the 'How' of wealth management – how to invest, how to grow, how to deploy capital. And to be clear, great talent and creativity are to be found on the side of those who design and promote the innovative financial structures and tools of wealth management. But before one can effectively execute on the 'How', one must first be clear regarding the 'Why' and with it a single question: what is the purpose of capital?

2. The purpose of capital, redefined[1]

Open the business section of any newspaper, tune into any financial news channel and watch the numbers move endlessly across the 'crawl', or ask any traditional wealth adviser: the purpose of capital is clear. As taught in leading business schools around the globe, the purpose of capital is to seek its 'highest and best use' – by which we mean that the appropriateness of any investment opportunity is assessed based on the degree to which it will optimise the greatest amount of financial return in exchange for any given measure of risk, return and liquidity.

Simply put, the purpose of capital is to make more capital.

For the past four centuries, an understanding of the purpose of capital as being a question of growth has been central to Western society's approach to economics, finance and wealth management. That understanding is the fundamental premise of modern Western financial capitalism, and in turn drives our approach not only to

"As taught in leading business schools around the globe, the purpose of capital is to seek its 'highest and best use'."

commerce and trade, but also to politics, social policy and environmental regulation. While the first question that one might ask upon meeting a new acquaintance may be, "What do you do?", the first thought may then also be, "I wonder how much they make? I wonder how much they are worth?"

In the main, when it comes to money, more is always thought to be better and the purpose of capital is to expand, grow and self-replicate. This understanding has been extremely successful when assessed on the basis of traditional measures of performance such as gross domestic product and when one considers the overall amount of financial wealth created in recent generations. We are witnessing the greatest process of wealth creation than in any decades before – much less centuries! More wealth, more millionaires – more billionaires! – and more money are moving around the world at lightning speed than at any other time in human history. If our measure of the purpose of capital is the creation of ever-greater amounts of wealth, we are most certainly on the right track.

And yet, we also know that something is amiss. When we are completely truthful and consider not only our individual and family wealth, but also our world's wealth, we must acknowledge that we have somehow, in the midst of our success, gone off-kilter. Our focus on making more money, our obsession with capital's purpose as self-replication, has taken our life and world's focus away from greater questions of what that wealth might ultimately be for and whether, in the creation of that wealth, we have run roughshod over those things that we value more than money. This narrow focus is something which the rising next generation continues to question as we then also consider:

- our climate crisis and access to fresh air and water;
- our health, both mental and physical;
- our belief that opportunity for self-improvement and personal advancement should be available to all; and
- our ability to go to sleep at night knowing that our wealth is not destroying the very things that we profess to care most about.

The purpose of capital as wealth growth is, in truth, a means to an end. It is the pursuit of money as a tool, but it is a vision of our task – our deeper meaning and purpose – that we must maintain as our North Star. We must understand capital's purpose as to support our life quest and not the success of wealth management as assessed on the basis of financial growth alone. As the author Edward Abbey observed: "Growth for growth's sake is the ideology of a cancer cell."[2]

"The purpose of capital as wealth growth is, in truth, a means to an end. It is the pursuit of money as a tool, but it is a vision of our task – our deeper meaning and purpose – that we must maintain as our North Star."

How did we come to this place where we thought we might consider wealth and capital as economics and finance, in the absence of considering the social and environmental aspects of capital? We have arrived here as a function of our understanding of the nature of value as grounded in the idea that value may be bifurcated: you either make money or you give it away. You must seek to do well or do good. You invest or you make a grant. You must choose between a career spent in 'do-gooding' non-profits (always said nicely, but with a faint tone of disparagement) or in the company of mercenary capitalists (ditto). And so on.

This understanding of capital, organisations and lives sets us in a place of separation where we believe we may operate with reference to financial and economic factors in the absence of considering social or environmental components of value. Those are something else, viewed as 'other' and removed from our consideration of investing. Too often, in too many realms of our lives, we take as reality the economic assumption of 'externalities' – namely, that those things that cannot be easily assessed on financial or quantitative terms should not enter into our calculation of what something is worth, of what its value is.

When considering an investment, we include the market value of a forest that is clear-cut and processed, but not the deeper value of the watershed that is then destroyed. As individuals, we believe (and we as a society then come to believe) that value can be disaggregated, divided and allocated in parts, as opposed to understanding value as fundamentally whole and non-divisible. Yes, we can consider the economics of a given thing, but we must also assess the extra-financial components of value; and the process of creation for value is itself a blend of elements with diverse components interacting and weaving along the trajectory of a strand of DNA – social, environmental and financial components inextricably one. This is the foundation of our understanding of 'blended value',[3] and is in turn the foundation of our understanding of the elements of value and purpose of our wealth that go well beyond money as simply capital and cash to be spent or invested in pursuit of ever-greater financial returns.

As we come to operate within a more holistic, blended understanding of the nature of value, we then also see that the lines which separate doing well and doing good, making money and creating value, are in fact false divides and artificial limits that we place on ourselves and our wealth. We recognise the purpose of capital as simply a social construct lodged within a set of interlocking assumptions that we have inherited from prior generations who were not themselves exactly wrong (as they were operating within the assumptions and constructs of their own day), but whose understandings of value and the purpose

"Past thinking with regard to how we should define the role and place of money in our lives and world is in many ways not relevant to the challenges of today, as many members of the rising next generation widely recognise."

of capital – when viewed from the perspective of today's lives – are inadequate, limiting and in some ways antithetical to the understanding of present generations. Past thinking with regard to how we should define the role and place of money in our lives and world is in many ways not relevant to the challenges of today, as many members of the rising next generation widely recognise. Yes, we must certainly understand how we got here and how capital moves within the existing systems that our elders have created. But we are ourselves called to promote a new set of assumptions and social constructs that succeeding generations will find most useful in their pursuit of the sustained, deeper value that we must now create.

It is up to each generation to reflect upon and define the purpose of capital anew, shaping a renewed understanding of that purpose and promoting a refreshed vision of capital's place in our world. And it is up to each of us – first as individuals, then as members of families and communities acting as global citizens – to evolve a dynamic understanding of capital's purpose because, in the words of historian Arnold Toynbee, "Civilizations die by suicide, not by murder."[4] Our decisions regarding wealth management and the purpose of capital are made not by others, but by our own good selves. And it is up to each of us to deepen our personal understanding of capital's place and purpose in our life so that we might not simply save ourselves, but prevent the death of our planet, humanity and those we claim to care most about.

3. The definition and role of impact

So then, value is a blend, consisting of economic, social and environmental components. And by extension, capital's purpose is less about an either/or approach to wealth management (make more or give more away) than it is a question of optimising its total performance. But what is the nature of total performance? What does a holistic approach to wealth and its management look like? How does the rising next generation understand the impact of our capital if its performance is assessed as more than financial, but social and environmental as well?

In recent years, increasing numbers of wealth holders have begun to deploy their wealth with an eye towards consideration of extra-financial performance, personal values and beliefs, and a commitment to having a net positive impact on the planet and its communities and ecosystems. While many believe these ideas and practices to be new, they have a long history. One may start the clock at any of a number of points. For our discussion, we will begin in 1604 at the dawn of modern financial capitalism, with the creation of the first publicly traded stock company, the Dutch East India Group. Having successfully raised capital from a diverse set of investors committed to its proposed venture of trade, the company financed an expedition. Upon its return, it was discovered that the firm had engaged in war and piracy instead of commerce. Several investors objected, selling their shares and initiating a campaign challenging the board of governors in the belief that the terms on which their investments had been received had been violated – and that the practices of the expedition conflicted with their religious beliefs. Thus, the debate regarding the purpose of capital and corporation began.

Moving ahead a few centuries, in the 1960s, we saw a new generation of wealth holders and fiduciaries seek to screen out companies thought to be operating in ways that conflicted with the beliefs of investors. These investors removed the 'sin stocks' of tobacco, alcohol and firearms from their portfolios – later adding defence industry companies supplying weapons of war used against the people of Vietnam. And later still, these strategies were used to apply pressure on the government of South Africa by those who sought to bring down that country's system of apartheid.

In the 1970s, with the creation of the Environmental Protection Agency in the United States and related agencies in countries around the world, companies were required to report on their levels of pollution. Investors began using that data to separate environmental wheat from chaff and identify environmental 'best in class' firms to invest in. Based on this work, in the early 2000s, we then saw the rise of environmental, social and governance (ESG) integration – the idea that ESG factors are material to the performance of firms and their ability to manage that off-balance-sheet risk material to their generating financial return. Investment firms began managing capital with consideration of ESG as a risk mitigation strategy to protect investor interests and be used as a competitive advantage, creating financial returns that could beat the benchmark and reward investors and diverse stakeholders. 'People, planet and profits' became the slogan of the day.

In the mid-1990s, a new type of asset owner – many coming out of the dot.com, tech and finance communities – began to reject the notion that, having created their wealth through business, they should then deploy that wealth through foundations and charitable organisations. These asset owners sought to draw as direct a line as possible between their investment of capital and their generation of positive value in the world – what came to be called 'impact'. As these practices evolved, groups of investors and visionaries began formalising the language and practices of investing in this way; and by the mid-2000s, what is now called 'impact investing' was born.

What is interesting to note is that while new to that generation of asset owner, the idea of investing for impact was not truly a new concept in and of itself. It was perhaps new to younger entrepreneurs bred in the boardrooms and incubators of the world's Silicon Valleys and Wall Streets; but in many cultures around the world, the idea of managing wealth to do more than make more money is a longstanding tradition. I recall giving a talk on blended value and what would become impact investing at the World Economic Forum in Davos, Switzerland, 20 years ago and having the first questioner – a successful European businessperson – stand to make the point that while these were great ideas and practices, this was how his family had sought to manage its business for over 150 years! And indeed, beyond examples within US and Western European society, First Nation, African, many Asian and other cultures around the world have long viewed capital as a tool to advance the more complex task of providing for individuals, communities and ecosystems.

In the end, the truth is that all capital (from philanthropic to concessionary to market rate) and all organisations (whether non-profit, for-profit, cooperative or hybrid) create impact. The challenge for us is to understand what type of net positive impact we are creating and then to manage that impact in an intentional, strategic and transparent manner. How do we define this impact?

Many investors deploy capital that creates what may be thought of as 'ignorant impact'.[5] These investors simply do not know what they are invested in or how that capital translates to impacts (whether positive or negative) within companies, communities or ecosystems. Others may invest in 'cheap impact' – claiming that since they create a job or pay a tax, they are generating impacts of value to society. And yes, that is impact; but it is incidental and something created through the execution of their traditional business strategy. Such impact is not managed with intentionality. Workers come and go; and while we may claim that "Our people are our greatest asset", when the next downturn comes, they transform from asset to cost centre and are relieved of their duties.

This brings us to a key consideration, in that asset owners exploring the possibilities of impact investing must manage their wealth with awareness concerning where their capital is invested and the nature and types of impacts it is generating. As the saying goes, "Know what you own!" That said, we must never confuse intent with impact. It is fine to invest in a fund that is branded as socially responsible or of positive impact; but as responsible fiduciaries of capital, we have to dig beneath the marketing if we are to understand the true nature of the impact that we are creating and the degree to which it is advancing net positive impact.

"First Nation, African, many Asian and other cultures around the world have long viewed capital as a tool to advance the more complex task of providing for individuals, communities and ecosystems."

We may also reflect on the degree to which our capital creates broad impact or deep impact. 'Broad impact' may be thought of as the impact of an education or health initiative or medical research that potentially touches thousands of lives; versus the 'deep impact' of a regional-level education or health and wellness strategy that may touch the lives of only hundreds of people within a defined area, but that does so in a holistic manner through which individuals, families and the wider neighbourhood participate in and benefit from a set of investments.

As we will explore below, when discussing how investors might manage all their assets on an impact basis, there is no single response to the question of what the best way is to deploy capital for impact. The correct strategy (or more likely, set of strategies) is a question of one's understanding of legal fiduciary duty and our personal understanding of effective stewardship. The correct strategy is a function of our definition of the purpose of our wealth combined with our individual vision and goals. However, what is required of us as stewards of wealth is that we not accept the thinking and practices of traditional finance, which seek to convince us that our only measure of value is financial return, or that the size of our asset base is the value and legacy of our having lived a life.

"What is required of us as stewards of wealth is that we not accept the thinking and practices of traditional finance, which seek to convince us that our only measure of value is financial return."

4. Mutual impact

When we think about impact, most likely we think about it as something that happens to the other; something that we do to other people or communities. We have impact – whether positive or negative – on a situation, on a person's thinking or on a community's wellbeing. We employ others and seek to have a positive impact via the creation of good jobs. We educate others; we vaccinate people; we save endangered species. We give someone money; we invest in a company; we contribute to a non-profit.

But impact is about more than what we might do to others.

At one level, we should be proud to have a positive impact on our world; but at another level, the value for us personally may be about more than what we do – it is about who we might become. In the non-profit sector, a common saying is that the person volunteering receives more from the act of contribution than the non-profit or individual beneficiary of our good and well-intentioned efforts. When we engage in an effort of impact – with our capital or our time – we position ourselves in relation to the object of our impact. We reach out beyond our own self. We connect with the other. And this is what 'mutual impact' is all about.

In our efforts to make a positive contribution through the deployment of our capital, in our focus on generating positive blended value, we open up the opportunity for us to connect, to reflect, to engage; and in that process, to be transformed ourselves from the act of investing our resources, whether financial or otherwise. We open ourselves up to the possibility of becoming more than who we were prior to our pursuit of impact. We learn and grow by lowering the wall between self and other, and by seeking to be more fully present in our own lives as well as in the lives of those around us. This approach has been embraced by many members of the rising next generation as they seek to find a pathway and connect beyond what they might do for others.

In the past, who we were during the week was one thing and who we were on weekends something else. Our professional self was one identity and our personal self another. "It's not personal; its business," was the old saying. "Bring your whole self to work," is the new mantra.

In the new world that we are creating today – and which the rising next generation will play an increasingly important role in shaping – as we seek to be more fully connected with our world, with our lives and with our wealth, we move well beyond what some Buddhist traditions refer to as the 'illusion of separation'. In truth, we are all connected. If all you care about is your family, think about those family members who are yet to come. Consider your family not just 50 or 100 years from now, but – as some Asian families do – 1,000 years from now. When you take what is truly the long view – the perspective of the 1,000-year family – who you are and how you should invest are functions of your connection with countless others yet to come. Your understanding of impact goes well beyond your personal interests or agenda to embrace future possibilities and prospects. You open yourself up to the potential of becoming more than your own self, wealth or asset management strategy to the potential of becoming more than what you were at the start of the day, the life or the financial reporting period. Mutual impact is about investing one's wealth to create deep, sustained value to the benefit of you and your family as you are connected over time with other families, communities, ecosystems and possible futures, all unknown to you at the start of your journey.

Mutual impact offers a vision (defined by you in co-creation with your family and diverse and many other stakeholders) of traditional understandings of wealth and capital management to position you to capture the full value of your investments. This value is in part financial, but perhaps in greater parts social, personal, environmental and spiritual.

An exploration of mutual impact positions you to think differently about capital, its purpose and its application. Your options become limited not by particular investment strategies, instruments or funds. Rather, your options become a function of your pursuit of more profound life goals, ambitions and possibilities. When investing your capital, you consider the financial elements of an opportunity, but also your broader long-term goals and priorities. You consider the total blended value that you seek to create over the course of a life. And in this way, you understand the need to mobilise all of your assets to generate the impacts you seek with the value you crave.

5. Total portfolio management: mobilising assets in pursuit of purpose

In previous times, how one made money was disconnected from what one did with the money one made. Building on the idea that investing was about profit maximisation and charity about doing good, assets were managed with simple consideration for optimising the amount of wealth that one might generate through investing. More recently, as we realise the consideration of environmental and social factors as material to our ability to generate sound, consistent financial returns, growing numbers of investors have sought to operate within more of a 'both/and' approach to investing, as opposed to an 'either/or' approach that requires us to surrender our values in exchange for financial returns. As growing numbers of investors recognise that all capital and companies create impact, interest has grown in managing

"Growing numbers of investors have sought to operate within more of a 'both/and' approach to investing, as opposed to an 'either/or' approach that requires us to surrender our values in exchange for financial returns."

all of one's assets with consideration of a fiduciary's interest in optimising total performance of one's capital portfolio. While in the recent past, investment decisions were assessed and evaluated on the basis of risk and return, in today's future, investors are investing on the basis of risk, return and impact.[6]

Total portfolio management[7] seeks to achieve the appropriate amount of financial return within any given asset class, as well as to optimise the nature and form of impact that each type of investment might generate.

As we consider this approach, it is important to understand that we are not (unless we choose to!) abandoning the accepted wisdom of traditional finance with regard to asset classes and the importance of diversifying portfolio investments. Under that traditional approach, most investment portfolios are constructed by assembling some mix of stocks, bonds, real estate, alternative assets and cash or cash equivalents. If the investor is deemed to have a higher risk tolerance, one might have a larger allocation to direct investments or venture stage funds and firms. If the investor is more conservative, then perhaps there will be greater exposure to real estate and fixed income (eg, bonds or various debt notes).

Within a total portfolio management strategy, one still seeks to deploy capital with consideration of the investor's appetite for risk and return. What is different is that we add the component of impact to the equation. When considering portfolio construction, we understand that in addition to having various risk and return possibilities, each investment across the capital continuum – from stocks to bonds to real estate to alternatives, cash and beyond – has not only a projected financial return, but also what could be considered to be an 'impact profile'. In assessing an opportunity, we would normally ask about historic financial track record, overall performance, types and forms of risk and any number of other factors. Within a total portfolio management approach, we ask all of those questions, but also seek to define the nature of impact by asking questions such as the following:

- What is the firm's impact thesis?
- What thematic area does the investment address (eg, gender issues, racial equity and social justice, climate crisis, sustainable oceans)?
- How is the investment's impact assessed, measured and managed?
- Does the investment structure (eg, terms, timelines) align with our own interests in long-term value creation, positive employment policies, non-extractive business practices and so on?

"There is no assumed trade-off between 'doing well' and 'doing good'. Our focus is on the overall value that the investor seeks to create. There is no presumed market-rate benchmark that we are trying to beat."

In this way, we take the investor's overall goals – financial, certainly, but also with regard to the nature of the impact that the investor seeks to create – and then populate a portfolio with a diverse and financially responsible set of investments consisting of funds, direct investments/holdings or any number of investment instruments and vehicles deemed as having the greatest potential to generate the overall total returns (financial, social and environmental) that the investor seeks to generate.

There are a few points worth considering here. First, when we consider a total portfolio management approach, we would include consideration of how the investor's philanthropic portfolio is structured and deployed, viewing philanthropic capital as a part of the overall portfolio – not separate from it. Again, in a traditional approach, philanthropy is what is considered after one has invested for financial return and destroyed the planet and its people. In this context, philanthropy is viewed as the risk capital of society, allowing investors to take risk, buy down risk or create a 'capital stack' wherein philanthropic capital may help to catalyse market and community opportunities that might otherwise not be possible.

Second, there is no assumed trade-off between 'doing well' and 'doing good'. Our focus is on the overall value that the investor seeks to create. There is no presumed market-rate benchmark that we are trying to beat. If we are considering an investment in a strategy that has market-rate comparable options (eg, a green real estate investment trust versus a traditional real estate investment trust), we would expect to generate a 'competitive' rate of financial return with an added impact 'wrap'. But when we consider the overall portfolio, we understand that the investor is the market. What that means, quite simply, is that it is the steward of capital – the fiduciary or principal – that determines what is a 'good' return. Whether the financial return is better or worse than the next investor's under consideration is completely irrelevant; the only thing that matters is the purpose of the capital as defined for this individual portfolio. Now, in reality, many investors fall into broad categories of interest – for example:

- family offices looking to generate a sustained level of financial return together with impact in a set of thematic areas (eg, micro-finance, sustainable agriculture, education);
- foundations seeking to generate annual financial returns to fund grant making while ensuring that their mainstream investments are not contributing to the creation of the problems that the grant making (much less the foundation itself!) seeks to address; and
- individual asset owners seeking to become fully invested in deep impact within a given time period.

Each of these types of investors – and many others too numerous to list – seeks to invest not simply to have a larger financial pie at the end of the quarter, but also to use their capital to advance whatever their vision of value creation may be. And just as is true in traditional investing, different investors have different appetites for diverse core and satellite capital investment strategies that advance various types of impacts in the world.

Third, while all investing involves a set of assumptions regarding what the future may bring and the construction of investment portfolios to reflect the particular needs and interests of the steward of capital, at its core, the creation of a total portfolio is not simply about looking from the inside out – from your perspective, priorities and plans for your financial goals and objectives, and then to the timeworn and predictable investment strategies, tactics and practices that you used to believe in. Instead, impact investing is about stepping beyond what you today believe to be true of your world and our society to embrace a holistic, historically aware, catalytic perspective of our future life and its meaning – a life and meaning that you are using your assets (in collaboration with others) to create.

Fourth, traditional investors often pride themselves on being able to identify investment opportunities that mainstream investors either overlook or view as too risky. For impact investors, the frontiers of emerging markets, renewables, evolving practices in agriculture or fisheries management, domestic emerging markets represented by historically under-resourced communities and so on represent potential areas of investment which, over time, offer not only compelling financial returns, but also significant extra-financial impact.

For example, in the early days of Building Resources across Communities[8] in Bangladesh, the notion of lending circles and the practice of lending debt capital directly to extremely low-income women were viewed as highly risky and a potential violation of fiduciary duty. Yet in later years, mainstream commercial lenders came to view micro-finance, green bond offerings, social impact bonds and other related impact investment vehicles as a credible way to invest in non-correlated assets and engage in diversified risk management, as well as the generation of consistent financial returns.

Fifth, over the past two decades, impact investing – now broadly defined as the investment of capital in pursuit of measurable financial, social and environmental returns – has grown from niche to mainstream. If one takes into account the broad diversity of strategies potentially included in impact investing (responsible investing, best in class, ESG integration, sustainable finance, blended finance and direct impact investing), globally there is now in the order of $30 trillion of

"Impact investing is about stepping beyond what you today believe to be true of your world and our society to embrace a holistic, historically aware, catalytic perspective of our future life and its meaning."

investment capital flowing into such investment approaches. Asset owners and fiduciaries would not be moving their capital into such investments if they were not satisfied with the returns being generated. And as a field, we now know how to invest for impact in ways that we might never have imagined 20 or 30 years ago. The future holds great promise not only for those who are wealth holders, but also – most importantly – for communities, ecosystems and stakeholder groups around the world.

6. In sum, wealth *does* have weight...

...But that weight may serve as the foundation upon which the rising next generation can build a better, more fulfilled and realised life. It is weight that, when managed appropriately and with consideration of the full legacy that we seek to leave, gives us grounding in pursuit of meaning and money. When understood in terms of the purpose of capital, blended value, impact investing and total portfolio management, wealth becomes a cornerstone upon which we then build a life well lived, in deep relation to our family, our future generations and a new world to come – just as over the years of our life, we may discover a deeper relationship with our own evolving selves.

Notes

1 Many of the ideas and concepts explored in this chapter, while written for this volume, are based on much longer treatments found in the author's previous writings. In particular, please see free e-book *The Purpose of Capital: Elements of Impact, Financial Flows and Natural Being*. The book and related reader resources may be found at www.purposeofcapital.org.
2 Edward Abbey, *The Journey Home: Some Words in Defense of the American West* (Penguin, 1991). Quote sourced from Goodreads, www.goodreads.com/quotes/21664-growth-for-the-sake-of-growth-is-the-ideology-of.
3 This perspective on both a bifurcated and blended value proposition was first introduced by the author in 2000, with various research papers, talks and initiatives following in the years since. Those papers and related materials are offered for free to the public on the Blended Value website, www.blendedvalue.org.
4 Quote sourced from Goodreads: www.goodreads.com/author/quotes/5458318.Arnold_Joseph_Toynbee.
5 The following discussion and the next on mutual impact summarise concepts and ideas found in "On Impact: From Ignorant to Mutual", the second chapter in Jed Emerson, *The Purpose of Capital: Elements of Impact, Financial Flows and Natural Being* (Blended Value Group Press 2018), p36.
6 See "Risk, Return and Impact: Understanding Diversification within an Impact Portfolio", Impact Assets Issue Brief #2, 19 November 2012, www.blendedvalue.org/blog-posts/risk-return-and-impact-understanding-diversification-and-performance-within-an-impact-portfolio.
7 See "Total Portfolio Management: Construction of an Impact Portfolio", Impact Assets Issue Brief #15, 18 October 2015, www.blendedvalue.org/blog-posts/total-portfolio-management-construction-of-an-impact-portfolio.
8 Located in Bangladesh, Building Resources Across Communities has worked since 1972 to expand economic opportunity to under-resourced communities and entrepreneurs.

About the authors

Charlie Bain
Managing partner, Digitalis
charlie.bain@digitalis.com

Charlie Bain is managing partner at Digitalis, an advisory company that specialises in online reputation management, crisis communications, digital privacy and risk. He is widely recognised as a leading expert in advising clients on their digital footprint and the effect this has on their reputation. During his career, he has helped a number of leading families, global corporates and prominent individuals to understand the nascent field of internet risk and digital crisis communications.

Charlie is on the advisory board of VALUEworks, a multi-family office based in Zurich; and a senior adviser to Dallington Associates, a company that offers specialist mentorship for the rising generation. In addition, Charlie has written for *The International Family Offices Journal* and was a contributor to the book *Advising the Wealthy Client* (Globe Law and Business, 2020), giving an insight into his experience advising family offices.

In 2021, Charlie was recognised as a top recommended specialist in reputation management by *Spear's Magazine*.

Jed Emerson
Managing director, global lead – impact investing, Tiedemann Advisors
jemerson@tiedemannadvisors.com

Jed Emerson is a strategic adviser to families and investment firms working to weave impact and purpose into their capital management and deployment strategies. Internationally recognised as a unique thought leader and innovator, he has been referred to as both the 'Godfather' and the 'conscience' of impact investing.

Emerson co-authored the first book on impact investing and wrote many of the early framing papers on the field. He introduced such concepts as social return on investment, total portfolio management (in which investors consider how best to optimise value from philanthropic, near-market and market-rate investing) and blended value. His eighth book, *The Purpose of Capital: Elements of Impact, Financial Flows and Natural Being*, is available in free digital format and has been translated into both Chinese and Spanish. He has held academic appointments at Harvard, Stanford and Oxford business schools and is currently a senior research fellow at the University of Heidelberg.

Paul Hokemeyer
Founder, Drayson Mews International
phokemeyer@gmail.com

Paul L Hokemeyer (PhD, JD) is a licensed marriage and family therapist, consultant and author of the ground-breaking book *Fragile Power* (Hazelden, 2019). A founding principal of the London-based Drayson Mews International, he is one of the world's foremost experts on resolving the complex, sensitive and highly nuanced mental health and relationship issues that arise among the world's most prominent families. He is listed as one of the world's top problem solvers in *Tatler*'s High Net Worth Address Book and was chosen by Harvard Medical School to represent the field of behavioural health in the first cohort of its Global Leaders in Health Care programme.

Dr Hokemeyer's work has been utilised by the World Economic Forum and featured in a wide range of academic and popular publications, including *The New York Times*, *The Wall Street Journal*, *Harvard Business Review Arabia*, *The Johns Hopkins Newsletter*, WebMD and *The Journal of Wealth Management.*

Iraj Ispahani
CEO, Ispahani Advisory
iraj@ispahaniadvisory.com

Iraj Ispahani is the CEO of Ispahani Advisory, which advises family businesses on business strategy, governance, people and education. The firm operates internationally and specialises in working with family and private businesses, private foundations and wealth owners. Iraj also serves as a group director and board member of the Ispahani Group, a family business headquartered in Bangladesh which marked 200 years in 2020.

Prior to joining the family business, Iraj held global and regional leadership roles in banking at JP Morgan and organisational development at Korn/Ferry. He also co-founded Cantos, an online corporate communications business, in 2001.

Iraj is chair of the Shakespeare's Globe Council; an independent trustee of the Standard Chartered Foundation; an adviser to UNICEF in the United Kingdom and Bangladesh; and a member of the UK Development Board of the ICRC. He was a founding adviser of the Responsible Family Business and Wealth Ownership programme created by Cambridge Judge Business School.

He is now a member of the advisory board, lecturer and facilitator of a new programme led by the Institute for Sustainability Leadership at Cambridge on Multi-Generational Leadership, equipping the world's most influential families to shape the 21st century.

Iraj was educated at Winchester College and holds a master's degree in international relations from Cambridge University and a bachelor's degree (with honours) from London University in politics and history.

Ed Lee
Co-founder, Bowbridge
ed@bowbridge.co.uk

Ed Lee is a director of Bowbridge, a consultancy firm which helps families and entrepreneurs to enhance and protect shareholder value throughout the business cycle. With extensive financial, operational and transaction experience, he focuses on the development and delivery of strategic initiatives and transitions such as succession and exit. Ed helps business owners to evolve strategy, enhance business operations, improve profitability and navigate risks.

Ed was previously a director in KPMG's market-leading private equity team, advising some of the highest-profile global funds on their M&A

activities. He left KPMG in 2017 to join Bonhams as special adviser, navigating the business through operational improvement, succession to non-family management and sale to new shareholders in 2018.

Alongside involvement in Bowbridge and his own family operations, Ed is a business strategy expert at Ispahani Advisory and has a portfolio of non-executive roles. Ed is a fellow of the Institute of Chartered Accountants in England and Wales.

Stefan Liniger
Chief executive, Kaiser Partner Wealth Advisors
stefan.liniger@kaiserpartner.com

Stefan Liniger is the chief executive of Kaiser Partner Wealth Advisors and a senior adviser at Ispahani Advisory. He obtained his doctor iuris at the University of Zurich and his LLM at Cornell Law School. He is a non-practising member of the Swiss Bar and holds a postgraduate diploma in psychosynthesis counselling awarded by the University of Middlesex.

As a long-term sparring partner, Stefan helps families and entrepreneurs to solve their strategic wealth challenges – including family, business and investment governance. He also serves as a board member of family businesses and acts as trustee, protector, executor and mediator. Prior to joining Kaiser Partner Wealth Advisors, Stefan was chief executive of Rothschild & Co's global wealth planning and trust business, after having created and led the wealth planning function at Goldman Sachs. Before that, he was a partner with the law firm Bär & Karrer in Zurich.

Philip Marcovici
Principal, The Offices of Philip Marcovici Limited
philip.marcovici@marcoviciasia.com

Philip Marcovici is retired from the practice of law and consults with governments, financial institutions and global families. He was a partner of Baker McKenzie, which he joined in 1982, and practised in the area of international taxation in Hong Kong and Zurich while with the firm. Philip has also practised law in New York and Vancouver, British Columbia. He retired from Baker McKenzie at the end of 2009.

The author of numerous publications, Philip is also the author of *The Destructive Power of Family Wealth* (John Wiley & Sons). Among others, Philip is a member of the Public Policy Committee of STEP and chairs its Responsible Stewardship of Wealth thought leadership group. He holds law degrees from Harvard Law School and the University of Ottawa (*magna cum laude*), and is admitted to practise in Hong Kong, the State of New York, the Province of British Columbia (retired), Canada, England and Wales.

Jessica McGawley
CEO and founder, Dallington Associates
Jessica@dallingtonassociates.com

Jessica McGawley is a consulting psychologist, family mediator and the CEO and founder of Dallington Associates, a specialist mentorship practice for the rising next generation. She holds an undergraduate degree in ethnomusicology and African culture; a postgraduate diploma in counselling and psychotherapy; and a master's in consulting psychology – psychodynamic and systemic approaches.

Prior to founding Dallington in 2015, Jessica spent seven years as head of operations for London-based consulting firm Oxford Place, where she focused on wealth transition to the next generation.

The youngest-ever board member of United Nations Women London in 2012, Jessica proudly set up its first mentoring scheme. She is a trustee of the Cassandra Learning Centre, a charity that focuses on supporting victims of domestic abuse; and a governor of the Mossbourne Victoria Park Academy in Hackney, London. Jessica is listed as one of the world's top problem solvers in *Tatler*'s High Net Worth Address Book.

Caroline Underwood
CEO, Philanthropy Company
caroline@philanthropycompany.com

Over nearly three decades, Caroline Underwood OBE has worked with philanthropic individuals and families to achieve positive change, as well as with a wide range of charities and cultural bodies in the UK and worldwide.

Caroline was awarded an OBE for charitable services in the 2017 Queen's Birthday Honours. She is a fellow of the Royal Society of Arts; a trustee of donor-advised fund Our Common Good; a governor of Britain's leading preparatory school, the Dragon School, Oxford; and former vice chair of UNICEF UK.

About Globe Law and Business

Globe Law and Business was established in 2005. From the very beginning, we set out to create law books which are sufficiently high level to be of real use to the experienced professional, yet still accessible and easy to navigate. Most of our authors are drawn from Magic Circle and other top commercial firms, both in the UK and internationally.

Our titles are carefully produced, with the utmost attention paid to editorial, design and production processes. We hope this results in high-quality publications that are easy to read, and a pleasure to own. Our titles are also available as ebooks, which are compatible with most desktop, laptop and tablet devices. In 2018 we expanded our portfolio to include journals and Special Reports, available both digitally and in hard copy format, and produced to the same high standards as our books.

In the Spring of 2021, we were very pleased to announce the start of a new chapter for Globe Law and Business following the acquisition of law books under the imprint Ark Publishing. We are very much looking forward to working with our new Ark authors, many of whom are well-known to us, and to further developing the law firm management list, among other areas.

We'd very much like to hear from you with your thoughts and ideas for improving what we offer. Please do feel free to email me at sian@globelawandbusiness.com with your views.

Sian O'Neill
Managing director
Globe Law and Business
www.globelawandbusiness.com

www.ingramcontent.com/pod-product-compliance
Ingram Content Group UK Ltd.
Pitfield, Milton Keynes, MK11 3LW, UK
UKHW050834190426
470095UK00006BA/67

9 781787 42502